FUN

Food

FAST!

225 BUILT-FOR-SPEED DISHES *that are* SIMPLY DELISH

HEARST BOOKS
New York

An Imprint of Sterling Publishing
1166 Avenue of the Americas
New York, NY 10036

ISBN 978-1-61837-120-1

GOOD HOUSEKEEPING

Jane Francisco............ *Editor in Chief*
Melissa Geurts............ *Design Director*
Susan Westmoreland ..... *Food Director*
Sharon Franke............ *Food Appliances Director*

Distributed in Canada by Sterling Publishing
c/o Canadian Manda Group, 664 Annette Street
Toronto, Ontario, Canada M6S 2C8
Distributed in Australia by Capricorn Link (Australia) Pty. Ltd.
P.O. Box 704, Windsor, NSW 2756, Australia

Cover and Book Design by Laura Palese
Illustrations (with the exception of page 9) by gravual.com

For information about custom editions, special sales, and premium and corporate
purchases, please contact Sterling Special Sales at 800-805-5489
or specialsales@sterlingpublishing.com.

Manufactured in China

2 4 6 8 10 9 7 5 3 1

www.sterlingpublishing.com

FUN *Food* FAST!

225 BUILT-FOR-SPEED DISHES *that are* SIMPLY DELISH

Contents

INTRODUCTION

Need breakfast on the run?
Impromptu brunch?
Last-minute dinner for friends?
Dessert in 20 minutes?

No matter what your nine-to-five job description, you're a time manager. You juggle work, family, *and* a social calendar, so finding the time to grocery shop, prep, and cook can tax anybody's balancing skills.

Enter *Fun Food Fast!* where life in the express lane doesn't have to mean grabbing take-out. We've put together 225 of our favorite deliciously simple recipes, all with a minimum of ingredients and no more than 30 minutes prep time. To make this your new go-to cookbook, we added kitchen tricks, time saving hacks, and complete menus. In every chapter you'll find Punch It Up ideas that take a store-bought product (everything from bagels to meatballs) and offer a few creative ways to use it. The Go Fresh logo calls out riffs on melons, tomatoes, corn, zucchini and more. Build-a-Dish features a "keeper" of a recipe (think pancakes, mashed potatoes, burgers, classic vinaigrette), plus flavor variations. And these are only the start!

Our Mmm Morning chapter dishes out a simple avocado toast, sweet and savory bagel toppers, Cherry-Pecan Granola—all fabulous ways to start your day. If you're serving brunch, we give menu options, including Crustless Tomato Pie that would wow any guest. Flash Bites & Beverages offers tasty dips (I love the New York Bagel Dip), plus snack and adult beverage options for impromptu entertaining. If you're in the mood for a super-fast Broccoli-Cheddar Soup, Easy Minestrone, or a classic Iceberg Wedge, check out Speedy Soups & Sides.

Consider Master Your Mains your personal life-saver, adding to your chicken repertoire, suggesting company-worthy recipes with only 15 minutes of prep, or making you a hero in your mac-'n'-cheese–loving family's eyes.

If you're wondering how to round out that something on the grill or roast chicken, Side Attractions gives you the lowdown on gussying up sweet potatoes, 'shrooms and quinoa, as well the usual suspects. And, finally, Sugar Rush scores big with a No-bake Chocolate Tart, Skinny Shortcake Poppers, Banana Dream Pie and more.

In the *Good Housekeeping* Test Kitchens, our team develops, tests and, yes, tastes every recipe that carries the *Good Housekeeping* name. Is it a tough job? Sometimes. Is it a fun job? You bet! Every recipe is at least triple-tested, often more, to make sure it works on any stovetop, in any oven, with any brand of ingredients, no matter what. Our goal is to deliver delicious, easy-to-shop-for recipes that will make any meal a good one. As we tweak, we're also looking for ways to streamline recipes so you won't have to dirty every pot in the kitchen just to get dinner on the table.

So sit down . . . choose a recipe for today, as we help you turn mealtime into fun time with your family.

Susan Westmoreland
FOOD DIRECTOR, GOOD HOUSEKEEPING

mmm
MORNING

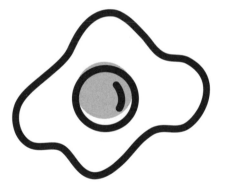

If you need a little *eggs*-tra
to fuel up this morning, we
offer just the fast fixes.

California Sunrise

TOAST

For extra crunch, sprinkle each toast with roasted hulled pumpkin seeds (*pepitas*).

PREP
15
min

SERVES
4

In medium bowl, mash **1 ripe avocado,** pitted, peeled, and cubed; **½ teaspoon fresh lemon juice; ¼ teaspoon salt;** and **¼ teaspoon crushed red pepper.** Heat **1 tablespoon olive oil** in large nonstick skillet over medium heat. Crack **4 large eggs** into skillet and cook **1 MINUTE** or until whites set around edges. Cover skillet; cook **2 TO 3 MINUTES** longer or until whites set completely. Meanwhile, toast **4 slices whole-grain bread;** top evenly with avocado mixture. Divide eggs among toasts.

KITCHEN HACK

Crack eggs into individual cups or small bowls, then slide each one into the hot skillet.

PUNCH IT UP!
Toasted Bagels

CLASSIC NEW YORK BAGEL

Harsh-tasting raw onion? Rinse slices under cold water, then pat dry with paper towels.

Spread **1 tablespoon softened cream cheese** on **1 toasted bagel half;** top with **1 slice lox or smoked salmon, a few thin slices red onion,** and **1 tablespoon roughly chopped fresh dill.**

....

CHOCOLATE-BANANA TREAT BAGEL

Works great with chocolate peanut butter too.

Spread **1 tablespoon chocolate-hazelnut spread** on **1 toasted bagel half;** top with **½ sliced banana,** and **2 tablespoons toasted flaked sweetened coconut.**

Enjoy our 5-minute toppers on toasted bialys, sliced rustic bread, or English muffins if you prefer. All recipes make 1 serving.

GROWN-UP PIZZA BAGEL

Set rack 5 inches from heat source and preheat broiler. Sprinkle **½ cup cubed fresh mozzarella cheese** on **1 toasted bagel half;** broil **1 TO 2 MINUTES** to melt slightly. Top with **½ cup halved grape tomatoes, 1 tablespoon torn fresh basil leaves, 1 teaspoon olive oil,** and **⅛ teaspoon salt.**

....

SWEET RICOTTA-STRAWBERRY BAGEL

No ricotta on hand? Swap in cottage or farmer cheese.

Spread **¼ cup ricotta cheese** on **1 toasted bagel half;** top with **2 sliced strawberries** and **1 teaspoon balsamic vinegar** mixed with **½ teaspoon sugar.**

Classic New York Bagel

Grown-Up Pizza Bagel

Chocolate-Banana Treat Bagel

Sweet Ricotta-Strawberry Bagel

Berry-Avocado
SMOOTHIE

Using berries straight from the freezer ensures this smoothie will be extra-thick.

PREP
5
min

SERVES
4

In blender, puree **1 ripe avocado,** pitted and peeled; **2½ cups orange juice; 2 cups frozen mixed berries; 2 cups packed baby spinach;** and **2 cups ice cubes** until smooth and frothy.

BUZZ, BUZZ

Breakfast smoothies are as simple as a flick of the wrist when you follow these steps.

USE CHILLED INGREDIENTS This will keep your smoothie frosty longer.

CRUSH OR BREAK ICE (IF USING) Make it the final ingredient you add to the container for the best consistency.

RUSH IT Ready to whirl? Bypass the low or stir button and go straight to high speed. Your smoothie will be thicker.

STRAWBERRIES & CREAM
Smoothie

A mere ¼ cup vanilla frozen yogurt is the secret ingredient in this extra-luscious smoothie.

PREP
10
min

SERVES
2

In blender, puree **1 pound strawberries,** hulled; **1 cup frozen peach slices;** ¼ **cup vanilla frozen yogurt;** ¼ **cup milk;** and **2 tablespoons honey** until smooth.

KITCHEN HACK

Insert a plastic straw into the pointed tip of each strawberry and push it through the center. The hull and green cap will pop right off.

Strawberries & Cream Smoothie

TROPICAL
Smoothie

Swirl in ½ teaspoon grated peeled fresh ginger for even more tropical punch.

PREP
10
min

SERVES
2

In blender, puree **1 pound nectarines,** sliced; **1 cup frozen mango or pineapple chunks;** ½ **cup apple juice;** and ½ **cup vanilla yogurt** until smooth and frothy.

Cheesy
CHIVE
OMELET

Feel free to sub in any fresh tender herb you have handy for the chives, like basil, parsley, or tarragon.

PREP	SERVES
5	**1**
min	

In small bowl, with wire whisk, beat **2 large eggs,** *1 tablespoon water,* and **1/8 teaspoon salt.** Melt **2 teaspoons butter or margarine** in small nonstick skillet over medium heat. Add egg mixture and cook, pushing eggs toward center, **3 MINUTES** or until almost set. Top with **1 ounce cream cheese** and **2 teaspoons snipped fresh chives;** fold in half.

Crustless
TOMATO
PIE

By skipping the typical piecrust, this brunch-worthy dish takes just minutes to prepare.

PREP
20
min

SERVES
6

Preheat oven to 375°F. In large bowl, whisk together **½ cup milk** and **1 tablespoon cornstarch,** then whisk in **1 container (15 ounces) ricotta cheese, 4 large eggs, ½ cup chopped fresh basil, ½ cup freshly grated Parmesan cheese, ¼ cup sliced green onions,** and **½ teaspoon salt.** Pour egg mixture into 10-inch nonstick oven-safe skillet; top with **1 pound tomatoes,** sliced. Bake **35 TO 40 MINUTES** or until set and puffed.

KITCHEN HACK

To test this pie for doneness, insert a small knife in the center of the skillet. It should come out clean.

Skinny FRENCH TOAST

Our lightened-up version of this morning classic is just as scrumptious as the original. Add ½ teaspoon grated orange peel to the egg mixture if you like.

PREP	SERVES
15 *min*	**4**

2 large egg whites
1 large egg
¾ cup low-fat (1%) milk
¼ teaspoon vanilla extract
⅛ teaspoon salt
2 teaspoons butter or margarine
8 slices firm sandwich bread

Maple syrup or honey

1. Preheat oven to 200°F. In pie plate, with wire whisk, beat egg whites, egg, milk, vanilla, and salt. In 12-inch nonstick skillet, melt 1 teaspoon butter over medium heat.

2. Dip bread slices, 1 at a time, in egg mixture, pressing bread lightly to coat both sides well. Place 3 or 4 slices in skillet, and cook **6 TO 8 MINUTES** or until lightly browned on both sides.

3. Transfer French toast to cookie sheet; keep warm in oven. Repeat with remaining butter, bread slices, and egg mixture. Serve French toast with maple syrup or honey, or one of our toppers, right.

KITCHEN HACK

Heat an electric griddle to 350°F and cook the French toast all in one batch.

BUILD A DISH

Consider our Skinny French Toast a blank canvas for a multitude of embellishments. Prepare the recipe as directed, add a 10 minute (or less) topper, and you'll never be bored. All recipes make 4 servings.

APPLE-BACON FRENCH TOAST

Use Granny Smith or Golden Delicious apples; they'll hold their shape best when cooked.

In microwave-safe bowl, microwave **2 peeled and sliced apples, 2 tablespoons brown sugar,** and **1 tablespoon maple syrup** on High **3 TO 4 MINUTES** or until soft. Stir in **3 slices cooked, chopped bacon.** Serve on French toast.

PEACHES 'N' CREAM FRENCH TOAST

In microwave-safe bowl, microwave **1 cup chopped frozen peaches, ½ cup peach preserves,** and **¼ teaspoon vanilla extract** on High **2 TO 3 MINUTES** or until warm. Serve on French toast; top with **whipped cream.**

MONTE CRISTO FRENCH TOAST

Top each slice French toast with **1 slice deli-sliced ham, 1 slice deli-sliced turkey, 1 slice deli-sliced Swiss cheese,** and **1 fried egg.** Sprinkle with **salt** and **freshly ground black pepper.**

NUTELLA™-BANANA FRENCH TOAST

In small microwave-safe bowl, microwave **½ cup chocolate-hazelnut spread** on High **1 MINUTE** or until melted. Top French toast with **2 small sliced bananas;** drizzle chocolate-hazelnut spread on top. Sprinkle with **flaky sea salt.**

BON JOUR, FRENCHIE!

Golden and crisp on the outside, moist and creamy inside, French toast is nothing less than breakfast heaven. Follow these tips to prepare this morning marvel like a pro.

CHOOSE firm, high-quality sandwich bread or challah bread. If you pick an unsliced loaf, cut it into ½-inch-thick slices.

SOAK the bread just 20 seconds on each side to ensure even saturation and prevent sogginess.

SPRAY the skillet with nonstick cooking spray, then melt the butter. This will help prevent the butter from burning.

Overnight FRENCH TOAST

Talk about a no-brainer! Pop this dish in the oven and you're good to go. Pair it with maple syrup and fresh berries or any of our French toast toppers (p. 21).

PREP
20
min

SERVES
4

Line large cookie sheet with parchment paper; grease with **1 tablespoon butter or margarine.** In pie plate, with wire whisk, beat **4 large eggs, 1 cup milk, 1 teaspoon vanilla extract, 1 teaspoon sugar, pinch ground nutmeg,** and **pinch salt.** Soak **8 slices hearty bread,** 1 at a time, in egg mixture; place on parchment paper. Cover with plastic wrap; refrigerate **1 HOUR OR OVERNIGHT**. Preheat oven to 450°F. Brush slices with **2 tablespoons butter or margarine,** melted. Bake **10 MINUTES**. Flip slices; bake **7 TO 8 MINUTES** longer or until golden.

Potato
OMELET

Pre-shredded cheese is a quick cook's morning must-have. While Cheddar is an all-time fave, swap in pepper Jack cheese or Mexican four-cheese blend if you like.

PREP
20
min

SERVES
4

In 10-inch nonstick skillet, heat **1 tablespoon olive oil** over medium heat. Add **2 cups thinly sliced onion; ½ pound baby potatoes,** thinly sliced; and **⅛ teaspoon salt.** Cover and cook **10 MINUTES** or until vegetables are tender, stirring occasionally. In large bowl, with wire whisk, beat **6 large eggs, 2 large egg whites, ½ cup shredded sharp Cheddar cheese,** and **¼ teaspoon salt.** Pour egg mixture into pan. Reduce heat to medium-low; cook **10 MINUTES** or until bottom is brown, pushing edges into center as they set. Place plate on top of skillet; invert. Slide omelet back into skillet, uncooked side down. Sprinkle with **½ cup shredded sharp Cheddar cheese.** Cover and cook **4 MINUTES** or until set. Cut into wedges and sprinkle with **sliced green onions.**

KITCHEN HACK

To separate the eggs, crack an egg into a small funnel set over a bowl. The whites will run through the funnel leaving the yolk behind.

Apple Granola Muffins

APPLE GRANOLA *Muffins*

All-purpose baking mix makes these muffins super speedy. Freeze any extras in a ziptight plastic bag up to 2 months.

PREP
20
min

SERVES
12

Preheat oven to 375°F. Line 12 muffin-pan cups with paper liners. In large bowl, combine **2 cups all-purpose baking mix** (such as Bisquick); **⅔ cup milk; ⅓ cup packed brown sugar; 1 large egg,** beaten; **2 tablespoons butter or margarine,** melted; **1 teaspoon vanilla extract;** and **½ teaspoon ground cinnamon.** Stir in **1 apple,** peeled and finely chopped; **½ cup granola,** crumbled; and **½ cup dried cranberries.** Divide among prepared muffin cups. Bake **15 TO 18 MINUTES** or until toothpick inserted in centers comes out clean. Cool completely on wire rack.

KITCHEN HACK

Use an ice-cream scoop to divide the batter among the muffin cups.

WHOLE-GRAIN *Muffins*

Pancake mix isn't just for pancakes! Adding fiber-filled dried plums (aka prunes) makes these muffins extra moist.

PREP
15
min

SERVES
12

Preheat oven to 375°F. Line 12-cup muffin pan cups with paper liners. In large bowl, with wire whisk, stir together **2 cups whole-grain or multigrain pancake mix, 1 cup milk,** and **1 large egg** until blended. Whisk in **¼ cup butter or margarine,** melted, and then **1 cup packed prunes,** finely chopped, just until combined. Divide batter among prepared muffin cups. Bake **25 MINUTES** or until toothpick inserted in centers comes out clean. Cool completely on wire rack.

KITCHEN HACK

Prep the prunes minus the mess by spraying the knife with nonstick cooking spray.

HUEVOS
Rancheros

Got cumin? Lightly sprinkle the eggs with a pinch after you crack them into the pan.

PREP
15
min

SERVES
4

KITCHEN HACK

To mash canned beans lickety-split, use a potato masher or a pastry cutter.

Rinse **1 can (15 ounces) pink beans;** drain well. Reserve ¼ cup beans in small bowl. In medium bowl, mash remaining beans with **¼ cup chopped fresh cilantro** and **2 tablespoons medium-hot salsa.** In 12-inch nonstick skillet, heat **1 tablespoon olive oil** over medium heat. Carefully crack **4 large eggs** into pan without breaking yolks. Cover and cook **4 MINUTES** or until whites set. Spread mashed bean mixture on **4 warm corn tortillas;** top each with 1 cooked egg, **2 tablespoons salsa,** 1 tablespoon reserved beans, and **1 teaspoon chopped fresh cilantro.**

CHILES RELLENOS *Pie*

With practically no chopping, this morning classic is a breeze to throw together. Put your personal stamp on the flavor by subbing in blue corn or black bean baked tortilla chips.

PREP	SERVES
15 *min*	**6**

Preheat oven to 350°F. Drain **2 cans (4 to 4½ ounces each) whole green chiles.** Slit each chile on one side; open flat and pat dry with paper towels. Grease 9½-inch deep-dish pie plate; line chiles on bottom. In large bowl, with wire whisk, beat **5 large eggs** with **1½ cups milk** and ½ cup finely chopped fully cooked **chorizo** (2 ounces); pour over chiles. Top with **2 cups coarsely crushed baked tortilla chips.** Bake **40 MINUTES** or until set in center.

LET'S DO BRUNCH!

If you're expecting guests this weekend, relax! We've got three simple menus plus a quickie dessert (just for fun).

MEXI BRUNCH
Tropical Smoothie (p. 16)
Huevos Rancheros (p. 28)
No-Cook Key Lime Pie (p. 226)

MARKET FRESH BRUNCH
Breakfast Peach "Crisp" (p. 35)
Crustless Tomato Pie (p. 18)
No-Cook Watermelon "Cake" (p. 223)

COMFORT FOOD BRUNCH
Piña Colada Yogurt (p. 30)
Monte Cristo French Toast (p. 21)
Easiest Baked Apples (p. 233)

NECTARINE &
TOASTED ALMOND YOGURT

Like it thick and creamy? Use a single-serve container of plain Greek yogurt!

On microwave-safe plate, microwave **2 tablespoons sliced natural almonds** on High **1 MINUTE** or until toasted. Mix **1 sliced nectarine** and **1 tablespoon brown sugar** in small bowl; spoon over 1 container yogurt. Top with almonds.

Take a 6-ounce container of plain-Jane yogurt, pick a jazzy riff, and in just 5 minutes add glam to your morning meal. All recipes make 1 serving.

BLUEBERRY &
GRAHAM CRACKER
YOGURT

Top 1 container yogurt with **¼ cup blueberries; ¼ cup cinnamon-flavored graham crackers,** crushed; **1 tablespoon honey;** and **¼ teaspoon vanilla extract.**

CHOCOLATE &
RASPBERRY YOGURT

Mix 1 container yogurt and **2 tablespoons chocolate-hazelnut spread** in small bowl; top with **1 teaspoon raspberry jam.** Garnish with **raspberries.**

PIÑA COLADA
YOGURT

On microwave-safe plate, microwave **¼ cup flaked sweetened coconut** on High **1 TO 2 MINUTES** or until toasted. Top 1 container yogurt with **½ cup chopped pineapple** and coconut.

Mediterranean PARFAITS

Honey and pistachios give this morning treat a taste of the Aegean.

PREP
10
min

SERVES
4

Divide **1⅓ cups plain yogurt** among 4 glasses. Top evenly with **1 cup shredded wheat cereal,** crushed; **4 teaspoons honey;** and **8 teaspoons chopped shelled salted pistachios.**

KITCHEN HACK

Place the cereal in a ziptight plastic bag and crush it with a rolling pin.

BACON

USE THESE TIPS TO ENJOY BACON TO THE MAX.

Bacon is the stuff that gets people out of bed in the morning: Its smoky aroma and salty, yet subtly sweet bite screams, "Eat me!"

CHOOSE CENTER-CUT BACON You'll get that big, bold bacon taste for approximately one less gram of total fat per strip (translation: more smoky meat).

TRY TURKEY BACON Made up of smoked and ground turkey, this bacon is reformed to resemble strips. Since turkey bacon doesn't have as much fat as pork bacon, you'll get less shrinkage when cooked.

WATCH THE FLAME If you've been burned by skillet bacon that turns out tough and brittle rather than uniformly crisp and tender, use controlled, moderate heat.

Maple-Glazed
BLACK PEPPER BACON

Good ole bacon is slathered with maple syrup and black pepper, then baked on a rack to crisp perfection.

PREP	SERVES
5 *min*	**4**

Preheat oven to 400°F. Arrange **8 slices thick-cut bacon** on rack fitted into jelly-roll pan. Brush slices with **3 tablespoons maple syrup;** sprinkle with **½ teaspoon coarsely ground black pepper.** Bake **15 TO 20 MINUTES** or until crisp.

Bacon-Cheddar
QUICHE

This speed-demon version of classic Quiche Lorraine has luscious creamed corn in every bite.

PREP	SERVES
15 *min*	**6**

Preheat oven to 350°F. Place **9-inch frozen deep-dish piecrust** in its pan on cookie sheet; bake **15 MINUTES.** In medium bowl, with wire whisk, beat **3 large eggs** and **1 can (14¾ ounces) creamed corn.** Pour into crust; top with **¼ cup cooked chopped bacon** and **½ cup shredded Cheddar cheese.** Bake **45 MINUTES** or until set in center.

Savory
SCONES

Serve simple scrambled eggs with these bacon-studded scones.

PREP	SERVES
15 *min*	**10**

Preheat oven to 450°F. Line large cookie sheet with parchment paper. In 12-inch skillet, cook **6 slices bacon** over medium heat **4 MINUTES** or until crisp. Drain on paper towels; crumble. Transfer bacon and ¼ cup fat to large bowl. Mix in **2 cups all-purpose flour, 1 tablespoon baking powder, ¼ cup finely chopped green onions, ¼ teaspoon salt,** and **¼ teaspoon freshly ground black pepper.** Stir in **¾ cup milk.** Drop by heaping tablespoons onto prepared cookie sheet. Bake **12 MINUTES** or until golden brown.

Cherry-Pecan
GRANOLA

This recipe doubles easily so stock up. Stash the extras in an airtight container at room temperature up to 1 month.

PREP
15
min

MAKES
4
cups

Preheat oven to 400°F. Line a 15½″ by 10½″ jelly-roll pan with parchment paper. In large bowl, toss together **2 cups old-fashioned oats,** uncooked; **1 cup chopped pecans; 3 tablespoons olive oil;** and **2 tablespoons warm honey** until well coated. Spread in single layer in prepared pan. Bake, stirring once, **10 MINUTES** or until golden brown. Cool completely in pan on wire rack. Toss granola with **1 cup dried sweet cherries.**

KITCHEN HACK

Measure the oil first, then the honey—that way it will slide right off the measuring spoon without the sticky mess.

Breakfast

PEACH "CRISP"

This morning riff on a dessert classic relies on summer-ripe peaches to keep the sweetness level in check.

PREP
10
min

SERVES
4

In large microwave-safe bowl, toss **1 pound peaches,** sliced; **1 tablespoon maple syrup; 1 teaspoon vanilla extract;** and **⅛ teaspoon ground cinnamon.** Microwave on High **4 MINUTES** or until tender and juicy. Divide among 4 bowls; top evenly with **½ cup granola** and **1 cup plain yogurt.**

Classic
PANCAKES

Pile on the fresh fruit! Dress up these lighter-than-air pancakes with whatever is fresh and seasonal, from peaches and raspberries in summer to sliced banana and kiwifruit in winter.

PREP
20
min

SERVES
3

1 cup all-purpose flour
2 tablespoons sugar
2½ teaspoons baking powder
½ teaspoon salt
1¼ cups milk
1 large egg, lightly beaten
3 tablespoons butter or margarine, melted
1 tablespoon vegetable oil

**Softened butter or margarine
    and maple syrup**

1. In large bowl, with wire whisk, stir flour, sugar, baking powder, and salt. Add milk, egg, and butter and stir just until flour mixture is moistened.

2. Heat griddle or 12-inch skillet over medium heat until a drop of water sizzles; brush lightly with oil. Pour batter by scant ¼ cups onto hot griddle, making about 4 pancakes at a time. Cook **2 MINUTES** or until tops are bubbly, some bubbles burst, and edges look dry. With wide spatula, turn pancakes and cook **2 MINUTES** longer or until undersides are golden. Transfer pancakes to platter. Cover; keep warm.

3. Repeat with remaining batter, brushing griddle with more oil if necessary. Serve pancakes with softened butter and maple syrup.

If our tasty flapjacks won't make you flip, these foolproof spin-offs certainly will. Prepare the batter as directed—then try these 5-minute stir-ins and toppings. All recipes make 3 servings.

STRAWBERRY-ALMOND PANCAKES

Stir **¼ cup sliced almonds** and **¼ teaspoon almond extract** into pancake batter. Top with **sliced strawberries** and **confectioners' sugar.**

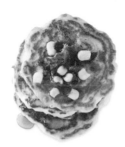

BACON-CORN PANCAKES

Use fully cooked bacon!

Stir **3 slices cooked crumbled bacon** and **½ cup corn kernels** into pancake batter. Drizzle with **maple syrup.**

PEANUT BUTTER–BANANA PANCAKES

Stir **½ cup chopped banana** and **⅓ cup peanut butter chips** into pancake batter. Top with **banana slices;** drizzle with **honey.**

DOUBLE CHOCOLATE PANCAKES

Stir **⅓ cup chocolate chips** and **2 tablespoons unsweetened cocoa** into pancake batter. Top with **whipped cream** and **chocolate sauce.**

PANCAKE RULES

Follow these 3 steps for perfect pancakes every time.

1. AVOID OVERMIXING THE BATTER Whisk just until the flour streaks have disappeared, leaving the lumps. If you overmix, gluten will develop from the flour, making your pancakes chewy instead of fluffy.

2. LET THE BATTER REST 5 MINUTES That's the time it takes the flour to absorb all the liquid so it sets up properly. Skip this step, and the pancakes will run together in the pan.

3. MAKE A TEST PANCAKE TO CHECK THE HEAT Drop a tablespoon of batter in the center of the preheated pan; cook I minute. If it's golden brown on the bottom, you're good to go. If it remains blond—or is close to burning—adjust the heat accordingly.

Flash Bites

&

BEVERAGES

Starters, snacks, spreads—and more—
share one thing in common: speed.

Mini
SALMON CAKES

Cornflakes (yes, the breakfast stuff) give this elegant app a subtle nutty flavor and fabulous crunch.

PREP
25
min

SERVES
9

In food processor, with knife blade attached, pulse **1 pound skinless salmon fillet,** cut up; **1½ cups cornflakes; 1 teaspoon finely grated orange peel; 2 tablespoons fresh cilantro leaves; ½ teaspoon salt;** and **¼ teaspoon freshly ground black pepper** until finely chopped. Form into 9 patties. In 12-inch nonstick skillet, heat **1 tablespoon vegetable oil** over medium heat. Add cakes to skillet and cook, turning once, **9 TO 11 MINUTES** or until golden brown. Meanwhile, in small bowl, combine **1 navel orange,** peeled and diced; **2 tablespoons chopped fresh cilantro; ¼ teaspoon salt;** and **¼ teaspoon freshly ground black pepper.** Serve cakes with salsa.

KITCHEN HACK

To form the fish patties without sticky hands, dampen first with cold water.

Zap-Fast
POPCORN

Olive oil adds sophisticated flavor to microwave popcorn, so you can skip the extra step of melting butter.

PREP
5
min

SERVES
8

⅓ **cup popcorn kernels**
1½ **teaspoons olive oil**
Kosher salt

1. In large microwave-safe bowl, mix popcorn kernels and oil; cover with microwave-safe plate and cook on High **2 TO 3 MINUTES** or until popping slows.

2. Carefully remove plate; season to taste with salt and toss to distribute evenly.

KITCHEN
HACK

As soon as the kernels finish popping, uncover the bowl so the popcorn won't get soggy.

BUILD A DISH

Prepare our Zap-Fast Popcorn as directed, then choose from these 5-minute tasty twists. All recipes make 8 servings.

CURRY BUTTER POPCORN

Start with a bag of microwave popcorn! Just use plain or lightly salted (not buttered) for best flavor.

In small bowl, mix **2½ tablespoons melted butter or margarine** and **2 teaspoons curry powder;** toss with popped popcorn.

PARMESAN-HERB POPCORN

In small bowl, mix **2½ tablespoons olive oil, 1 tablespoon chopped fresh rosemary, 1 teaspoon chopped fresh thyme,** and **¼ teaspoon salt;** toss with popped popcorn and **⅔ cup freshly grated Parmesan cheese.**

BACON-CHOCOLATE POPCORN

Toss popped popcorn with **5 slices cooked crumbled bacon** on jelly-roll pan; drizzle with **½ cup melted chocolate chips.** Refrigerate **15 MINUTES** or until chocolate sets.

TACO NIGHT POPCORN

In small bowl, mix **1½ tablespoons olive oil, 1 tablespoon chili powder, 1 tablespoon finely grated lime peel, ½ teaspoon ground cumin,** and **¼ teaspoon garlic powder;** toss with popped popcorn and **1 cup tortilla chip pieces.**

New York Bagel Dip

New York
BAGEL DIP

Layers of smoked-salmon cream cheese with "the works" make this the perfect party dip. Whip it up in minutes; you can also stash it in the fridge up to 4 hours ahead.

PREP
15
min

MAKES
3
cups

In medium bowl, mix **8 ounces smoked-salmon cream cheese, ½ teaspoon finely grated lemon peel, 2 tablespoons fresh lemon juice,** and **⅛ teaspoon freshly ground black pepper.** In 1-quart glass bowl, alternately layer cream cheese mixture with **2 cups pretzel sticks,** broken; **1 medium tomato,** diced; and **1 small bunch green onions** (green parts only), thinly sliced. Serve with **crudités** or **crackers.**

Warm
SPINACH DIP

A can of artichokes is the secret ingredient to this anything-but-ordinary dip. Be sure to use the full-fat sour cream so the dip doesn't break while baking.

PREP
15
min

MAKES
5¼
cups

Preheat oven to 425°F. In food processor, with knife blade attached, pulse **1 container (16 ounces) sour cream; 1 package (10 ounces) frozen chopped spinach,** thawed and squeezed dry; **1 can (13¾ to 14 ounces) artichoke hearts in brine,** drained; **½ cup freshly grated Parmesan cheese; 1 clove garlic,** minced; **½ teaspoon freshly ground black pepper;** and **¼ teaspoon salt** until combined. Transfer to 2-quart baking dish. Bake **18 TO 20 MINUTES** or until bubbling. Serve with **crackers.**

KITCHEN HACK Use a potato ricer to squeeze dry the thawed frozen spinach in seconds.

45

Skinny
BEAN DIP

Thanks to canned beans and jarred roasted pepper, this fat-free dip doesn't skimp on big flavor or luscious texture.

PREP
10
min

MAKES
1½
cups

In food processor, with knife blade attached, puree **1 can (15 ounces) pink beans,** rinsed and drained well; **¼ cup roasted red pepper; 1 tablespoon fresh lime juice; ½ teaspoon ground cumin;** and **⅛ teaspoon salt** until smooth. Spoon mixture into small bowl. Top with **chopped fresh cilantro.** Serve with **baked tortilla chips.**

Creamy
HUMMUS

Edamame replaces the usual chickpeas in this protein-packed dip (which also makes a great sandwich spread).

PREP
10
min

SERVES
4

In food processor, with knife blade attached, pulse **2 cups frozen shelled edamame,** thawed; **¼ cup fresh lemon juice;** *¼ cup water;* **1 clove garlic; ¾ teaspoon ground cumin;** and **¾ teaspoon salt** until coarsely chopped. Through feed tube, drizzle in **½ cup olive oil;** blend until smooth. Spoon mixture into small bowl; sprinkle with **paprika** and serve with **pita wedges.**

KITCHEN HACK To quick-thaw frozen edamame, place it in a colander and rinse under running cold water 1 minute, then drain.

Creamy Hummus

MELON

Summer's finest offers instant refreshment.

IS IT RIPE?

Don't play the waiting game. Use melon when it's ripe and ready. The reason? Melons continue to ripen after picking, with the flesh softening and the aromas and flavor getting more intense—but they don't get any sweeter.

In search of a fabulous tasting melon? Put those old wives' tales aside and use these smart guidelines.

CANTALOUPE Take a sniff. Smell for ripeness at the blossom end (opposite the stem area), it should have a noticeably sweet aroma.

HONEYDEW Shake the melon. You should feel the seeds rattling around. The blossom end should give slightly when pressed gently.

WATERMELON Look at the bottom. There should be a creamy yellow spot from where it sat on the ground and ripened in the sun.

MELON-AVOCADO
Salsa

This zesty salsa also is delicious with seedless watermelon.

PREP
15
min

MAKES
4
cups

In large bowl, gently mix **3 cups diced cantaloupe melon; 1 ripe avocado,** pitted, peeled, and diced; **¼ cup pickled jalapeño chiles,** finely chopped; **¼ cup diced red onion;** and **½ teaspoon salt.** Transfer mixture to medium bowl. Serve with **tortilla chips.**

HONEYDEW
Frappé

As honeydews ripen, the rind turns from green, to creamy white, to yellow. Avoid green fruit, and if you can only find white melons, use the greater amount of sugar in the recipe.

PREP
15
min

SERVES
4 to 6

In blender, puree **4 cups cut-up ripe honeydew melon, ¼ cup loosely packed fresh mint leaves, 2 tablespoons fresh lime juice** and **1 to 2 tablespoons sugar** until smooth. Add **3 cups ice cubes** and puree until thick and frothy.

MINTY MELON
Salsa

Serve this salsa atop grilled salmon or chicken.

PREP
15
min

SERVES
4

In medium bowl, mix **2 cups diced seedless watermelon; 1 cup diced cantaloupe melon; ¼ cup packed fresh cilantro leaves,** finely chopped; **2 tablespoons fresh mint leaves,** finely chopped; **1 jalapeño chile,** seeded and minced; **2 tablespoons fresh lime juice;** and **¼ teaspoon salt.**

FETA-WATERMELON
Stacks

The briny taste of feta cheese is the perfect foil for super-sweet watermelon.

PREP **20** *min*

SERVES **10**

Cut **1 small seedless watermelon** into 1-inch cubes (about 40). Top with **1 (16-ounce) block feta cheese,** cut into 1-inch squares (¼-inch thick), and **1 cup fresh basil leaves;** secure with toothpicks. Transfer to platter; sprinkle with **3 tablespoons olive oil, ¼ teaspoon kosher salt,** and ¼ **teaspoon freshly ground black pepper.**

KITCHEN HACK

Watermelon is easier to cut at room temperature. Use a sharp knife with a pointed tip (aka a chef's knife) for the cleanest cuts.

Watermelon
LEMONADE

DIY lemonade and sweet seedless watermelon make the perfect summer refresher.

PREP
10
min

SERVES
4

In blender, puree **5 cups (1-inch) chunks seedless watermelon, ½ cup fresh lemon juice,** and **¼ cup sugar** until very smooth. Refrigerate at least **1 HOUR** or until cold. Serve over **ice.**

Classic
MOJITO

This bubbly rum cocktail with lime and fresh mint can hold its own paired with the spiciest appetizer.

PREP
10
min

SERVES
1

In cocktail shaker, with wooden spoon, crush **6 sprigs fresh mint, 3 tablespoons fresh lime juice,** and **2 to 3 teaspoons superfine sugar.** Add **1 cup ice cubes** and **¼ cup golden rum.** Shake until well blended. Fill 1 tall glass with **ice cubes.** Strain drink into glass and top off with **½ cup plain seltzer or club soda.** Garnish with **fresh mint sprig** and **lime wedge.**

Watermelon Lemonade

Classic Mojito

LEMON Julep

Talk about pure refreshment! Don't wait until Derby day to enjoy this lemony concoction.

PREP
10
min

SERVES
6

In large pitcher, combine **2 cups fresh mint leaves** and **2 lemons,** sliced. With handle end of wooden spoon, mash mint and lemons. Stir in **6 cups lemonade** and **1 cup bourbon** (optional). Serve over **crushed ice** and garnish with **lemon wedges** and **fresh mint sprigs.**

KITCHEN HACK

If your blender doesn't have a button for crushed ice, wrap about 2 cups ice cubes in a clean kitchen towel and place on a cutting board. With a rolling pin or large metal spoon, whack the ice until coarsely crushed.

CITRUS Spritzer

Save time by preparing this bubbly beverage with seedless navel oranges.

PREP
10
min

SERVES
6

In large pitcher, stir together **4 cups orange juice; 4 cups lemon-lime seltzer; 2 oranges,** sliced; and **2 limes,** sliced. Refrigerate at least **30 MINUTES** or until chilled. Serve over **ice.**

STRAWBERRY Iced Tea

For quickest prep, use instant unsweetened iced tea mix.

PREP
15
min

SERVES
6

In large pitcher, stir together **1 pound strawberries,** hulled and sliced; **¾ cup sugar;** and *¼ cup water.* Let stand, stirring occasionally, **20 MINUTES** or until sugar dissolves. Add **8 cups unsweetened iced tea,** stirring to combine. Refrigerate at least **1 HOUR** or until chilled. Serve over **ice.**

Lemon Julep

Citrus Spritzer

Strawberry
Iced Tea

PUNCH IT UP!
French Fries

TEX-MEX FRIES

Our pick: thick and chunky jarred salsa.

Top fries with **⅓ cup store-bought salsa; ½ cup shredded Cheddar or pepper Jack cheese;** and **3 green onions,** white and light green parts only, thinly sliced.

....

TAPAS-STYLE FRIES

In small bowl, mix **⅓ cup mayonnaise; 1 tablespoon fresh lemon juice; 1 teaspoon hot paprika; ¼ teaspoon salt;** and **1 clove garlic,** crushed with press. Serve with fries, dusted with more **hot paprika.**

*Gourmet fries have never been easier! Bake 1 (16-ounce) bag frozen crinkle-cut French fries as directed on label (the baking time will be **20 to 25 minutes**), then try these delicious 10-minute spinoffs. All recipes make 8 servings.*

PARMESAN-HERB FRIES

Toss fries with **¼ cup minced fresh parsley; 3 tablespoons freshly grated Parmesan cheese; 1 tablespoon chopped capers; 1 teaspoon finely grated lemon peel; ¼ teaspoon salt;** and **1 clove garlic,** crushed with press.

....

CLASSIC CHILI FRIES

Heat **½ cup hot store-bought beef or vegetarian chili.** Top fries with chili; **¼ small white or red onion,** chopped; and **2 tablespoons sour cream.**

Tex-Mex Fries

Parmesan-Herb Fries

Tapas-Style Fries

Classic Chili Fries

KITCHEN HACK

For the crispiest fries, bake on a large cookie sheet with low or no sides; don't overcrowd, or the fries will steam.

SHRIMP-AVOCADO
Ceviche

Looking to give this recipe some extra kick? Discard only half the jalapeño seeds before chopping the chile.

PREP
15
min

SERVES
6

In large bowl, toss together **1 pound peeled and deveined cooked shrimp,** cut up; **3 green onions,** sliced; **1 ripe avocado**; pitted, peeled, and cubed; **1 jalapeño chile,** seeded and minced; **¼ cup fresh lime juice;** and **1 tablespoon chopped fresh cilantro.** Cover and refrigerate **1 HOUR** or until chilled. Divide among serving glasses.

Spicy
CRAB
DIP

While canned crabmeat is okay in a pinch, we think more flavorful fresh or frozen crabmeat is worth the extra coin. Look for it in plastic containers sold over ice in the seafood section at the supermarket.

PREP
15
min

SERVES
8

In large bowl, with mixer at medium-high speed, beat **1 package (8 ounces) cream cheese,** softened; **¼ cup milk; 2 teaspoons hot pepper sauce;** and **1 teaspoon fresh lemon juice** until smooth. Fold in **1 cup lump crabmeat,** picked over. Spoon into small bowl. Sprinkle with **paprika** and serve with **crudités** and **crackers.**

SALMON
Spread

Cream cheese, capers, and plenty of lemon transform a ho-hum can of salmon into a tasty spread. If you have any extras, try it on your morning bagel.

PREP
10
min

SERVES
8

In food processor, with knife blade attached, blend **1 can (14¾ ounces) pink salmon,** drained well, skin and bones removed; **6 ounces reduced-fat cream cheese; ¼ cup mayonnaise; 1 teaspoon finely grated lemon peel; 2 tablespoons fresh lemon juice;** and **¼ teaspoon freshly ground black pepper** until smooth. Spoon mixture into small bowl; stir in **2 tablespoons capers,** drained and chopped. Cover and refrigerate **3 HOURS** or until chilled. Serve with **crackers.**

PUNCH IT UP!
Green Salsa

ZIPPY PINEAPPLE SALSA

Use fresh peeled pineapple rings or chunks from the produce section at the supermarket.

In large bowl, combine salsa, **2 sliced green onions, 1 cup chopped pineapple,** and **1 minced chipotle chile in adobo.**

. . . .

SMOKY SWEET CORN SALSA

No smoked paprika on hand? Substitute ¼ teaspoon ancho chile powder.

In large bowl, combine salsa, **2 cups thawed frozen corn kernels, 1 cup quartered grape tomatoes,** and **1 teaspoon smoked paprika.**

———

Take a (16-ounce) jar of your favorite green salsa and in 10 minutes (or less) add pizzazz to your next batch of chips and dip. All recipes make 6 servings.

———

ROASTED RED PEPPER SALSA

In large bowl, combine salsa, **¾ cup chopped roasted red pepper, ¼ cup minced red onion,** and **¼ cup packed fresh basil leaves,** chopped.

. . . .

MINTED MANGO SALSA

In large bowl, combine salsa; **1 ripe medium mango,** pitted, peeled, and finely chopped; and **¼ cup packed fresh mint leaves,** chopped.

Roasted Red
Pepper Salsa

Smoky Sweet Corn Salsa

Minted Mango Salsa

Zippy
Pineapple
Salsa

KITCHEN
HACK

Serve atop grilled chicken
breasts or white fish fillets.

PUFF PASTRY

PUFF, THE MAGIC PASTRY

Fancy schmancy, but a supermarket staple, puff pastry bakes into gorgeous flaky layers for easy-to-make, irresistible appetizers. The most common brand is a 17¼-ounce box, which contains two sheets of frozen pastry. Here's how to handle it like a pro.

THAW COMPLETELY Plan ahead and stick the frozen pastry in the fridge overnight, or let it stand at room temperature until pliable, about 45 minutes.

UNFOLD GENTLY This will help prevent the pastry from cracking. If any tears or holes are visible—not a problem. Just moisten your fingers and gently squeeze the pastry back together.

WORK CHILLED Puff pastry is easiest to work with when it's cold. If the pastry gets too soft while you're rolling or cutting it, place it on a cookie sheet and return it to the fridge or freezer to quickly firm up.

PIGS in Cribs

Guests will devour these mini frankfurters all dressed up in flaky pastry. Use turkey franks if you prefer.

PREP
20
min

MAKES
28

Preheat oven to 400°F. Thaw **1 frozen puff-pastry sheet from 1 (17¼-ounce) box.** Unfold sheet and cut into 4 even strips. Cut each strip crosswise into 7 pieces and place 1 inch apart on 2 cookie sheets. Cut slit lengthwise in center of each rectangle; from **1 package (14 ounces) cocktail beef franks,** place 1 frank in each. Bake **15 MINUTES**. Meanwhile, in medium bowl, mix **2 cups sauerkraut,** drained, with **2 teaspoons caraway seeds.** Serve "pigs" with sauerkraut mixture and **Dijon mustard.**

Honeyed PEACH PILLOWS

Crisp, golden puff pastry rectangles are topped with warm peaches and honey, toasted pecans, and goat cheese.

PREP
25
min

SERVES
6

Preheat oven to 425°F. Thaw **1 frozen puff-pastry sheet from 1 (17¼-ounce) box.** Unfold sheet and cut into 6 rectangles; place 1 inch apart on cookie sheet. Bake **13 TO 15 MINUTES** or until puffed and golden. Meanwhile, in large, microwave-safe bowl, microwave **¼ cup honey** on High **1 MINUTE**. Stir in **1 pound peaches,** cut into wedges. On microwave-safe plate, microwave **½ cup pecan halves,** chopped, on High **2 MINUTES** or until toasted. Cut **1 log (4 ounces) goat cheese** into 6 slices. Top each pastry "pillow" with 1 slice cheese; top evenly with peach mixture and pecans.

Cheese
STRAWS

Serve this classic finger food solo with cocktails or as an elegant accompaniment to a green salad.

PREP		MAKES
30		**32**
min		

Preheat oven to 400°F. Line 2 (15½- by 10½-inch) jelly-roll pans with parchment paper. Thaw **1 box (17¼ ounces) frozen puff-pastry sheets.** Unfold sheets. On lightly floured surface, with floured rolling pin, roll each sheet into 12- by 15-inch rectangle. Brush sheets with **1 large egg,** beaten. Onto 1 sheet, sprinkle **¼ teaspoon salt** and **¼ teaspoon ground red pepper (cayenne),** then **6 tablespoons freshly grated Asiago cheese** and **6 tablespoons freshly grated Parmesan cheese.** Place remaining sheet, egg side down, on top of filling so edges of sheets line up evenly; roll to 13- by 16-inch rectangle. With pizza wheel or knife, cut crosswise into ½-inch-wide strips; place strips, 1 inch apart, in pans. Twist each strip several times. Bake **18 TO 20 MINUTES** or until golden. With spatula, carefully transfer to wire racks to cool completely.

CUCUMBER-MELON
Sangria

Sangria is best enjoyed icy cold. To cut the chill time in half, set the pitcher of sangria in a large bowl halfway filled with ice water then stick it in the fridge.

PREP
15
min

SERVES
6 to 8

In large pitcher, stir together **1 bottle (750 ml) dry white wine; ½ cup gin; ½ cup packed fresh mint leaves; ½ English cucumber,** sliced; **½ honeydew melon,** cubed; and **3 tablespoons superfine sugar.** Refrigerate **1 HOUR** or until chilled. To serve, top with **1 cup seltzer.**

Cucumber-Melon Sangria

Restaurant-Style
RED SANGRIA

This classic recipe tastes just as fabulous as dining out, but with a lot less sugar. Try it with a Garnacha from Spain or a California Zinfandel.

PREP	SERVES
15	**6** to **8**
min	

On tray, freeze **2 cups seedless grapes, 12 ounces blackberries,** and **12 ounces raspberries 2 HOURS** or until frozen solid. Meanwhile, in large pitcher, stir together **1 bottle (750 ml) dry red wine; 1 cup orange juice; ½ cup tequila; ¼ cup orange-flavored liqueur; 3 tablespoons superfine sugar;** and **1 orange,** sliced. Refrigerate **1 HOUR** or until chilled. To serve, add frozen fruit.

KITCHEN HACK

To make the superfine sugar, grind an equal amount of granulated sugar in a mini food processor.

Restaurant-Style Red Sangria

Tropical
FAUX-GRIA

This thirst quencher has all the fruity taste of sangria—minus the alcohol.

PREP
15
min

SERVES
6 to 8

In large pitcher, stir together **4 cups pineapple juice; 2 cups orange juice; 2 cups cream soda; 2 cups pineapple chunks; 1 medium orange,** sliced; and **½ green apple,** thinly sliced. Refrigerate **1 HOUR** or until chilled.

Tropical Faux-Gria

Rosé-White Peach
SANGRIA

Elderflower liqueur gives this sangria a delicate floral taste. Serve as an aperitif with Manchego cheese.

PREP	SERVES
15 *min*	**6 to 8**

In large pitcher, mix **1 bottle (750 ml) dry rosé wine; ½ cup elderflower liqueur** (such as St. Germain); **¼ cup brandy; 1 cup raspberries;** and **2 medium white peaches,** sliced. Refrigerate **1 HOUR** or until chilled.

KITCHEN HACK

If you can't find ripe peaches, sub in nectarines or plums.

Rosé–White Peach Sangria

Best
STUFFED
EGGS

For an extra-creamy filling
add a teaspoon of milk.

PREP
20
min

SERVES
6

SHELL JOB

*Follow these hints for perfectly peeled
hard-cooked eggs every time.*

BUY eggs 7 to 10 days ahead of cooking.
This chilling time allows the eggs to take in
air and helps separate the membranes from
the shell.

PEEL eggs right after cooling. Cooling causes
the egg to contract slightly in the shell.

TAP eggs on countertop until shell is finely
crackled all over, then hold the egg under
cold running water to help ease the shell off.

6 large eggs
¼ cup mayonnaise
⅛ teaspoon salt

1. In 3-quart saucepan, place eggs and enough
cold water to cover by at least 1 inch; heat over
high heat just to boiling, about **10 MINUTES**.
Immediately remove saucepan from heat and
cover tightly; let stand **14 MINUTES**. Pour off hot
water and run cold water over eggs until cool to
the touch. Peel eggs.

2. Slice eggs lengthwise in half. Gently remove
yolks and place in medium bowl; with fork,
finely mash yolks. Stir in mayonnaise and salt
until evenly blended.

3. Place egg whites in jelly-roll pan lined with
paper towels (to prevent eggs from rolling).
Spoon yolk mixture into egg-white halves.

Go stuff it! Getting creative with stuffed eggs takes just 5 minutes. Prepare the yolk filling as directed for our Best Stuffed Eggs, then select from these delicious twists. All recipes make 6 servings.

CRUNCHY CURRY STUFFED EGGS

Mix filling with **1 teaspoon curry powder** and **1 teaspoon fresh lemon juice.** Spoon into whites; top with **sliced almonds** and **snipped fresh chives.**

PESTO-BACON STUFFED EGGS

Mix filling with **2 tablespoons store-bought pesto** and **1 teaspoon fresh lemon juice.** Spoon into whites; top with **crumbled cooked bacon.**

CAESAR STUFFED EGGS

Mix filling with **2 tablespoons freshly grated Parmesan cheese, 2 teaspoons fresh lemon juice, ¼ teaspoon minced garlic,** and **¼ teaspoon freshly ground black pepper.** Spoon into whites; top with **freshly shaved Parmesan cheese.**

SMOKY CHIPOTLE STUFFED EGGS

Mix filling with **1 tablespoon chopped chipotles in adobo** and **½ teaspoon cider vinegar.** Spoon into whites; top with **chili powder** and **fresh cilantro leaves.**

GREEN EGGS

& Ham

Smoky ham and tangy capers make this version of stuffed eggs devilishly good.

PREP
15
min

SERVES
8

Slice **8 hard-cooked eggs** lengthwise. Transfer yolks to medium bowl; arrange whites on platter. Mash yolks until smooth. Stir in **¼ cup mayonnaise; 1 ounce finely chopped ham; 2 tablespoons capers,** drained, finely chopped; **2 tablespoons fresh parsley,** finely chopped; *1 tablespoon water;* and **¼ teaspoon freshly ground black pepper** until mixed; spoon into egg whites.

THERE'S AN APP FOR THAT

In a party mood but want to keep it easy? Think apps. Check out our trio of speedy menus, each with a signature cocktail.

POOL PARTY
Feta-Watermelon Stacks (p. 51)
Crunchy Curry Stuffed Eggs (p. 73)
Mini Salmon Cakes (p. 40)
Lemon Juleps (p. 54)

MOVIE NIGHT
Roasted Red Pepper Salsa (p. 62)
New York Bagel Dip (p. 45)
Steakhouse-Style Latkes (p. 79)
Citrus Spritzers (p. 54)

TGIF BASH
Creamy Hummus (p. 46)
Jalapeño Bites (p. 76)
Pigs in Cribs (p. 65)
Restaurant-Style Red Sangria (p. 69)

KITCHEN HACK

Place the egg filling in a ziptight plastic bag, snip off a small section of one corner and pipe the filling into the egg white halves.

75

JALAPEÑO
Bites

Guests will go bananas over these zesty apps.

PREP
10
min

SERVES
4

Set rack 5 inches from heat source and preheat broiler. Arrange **12 crackers** on 15½- by 10½-inch jelly-roll pan. Top crackers with **12 slices ripe banana** and **12 slices pickled jalapeño chiles**. Sprinkle evenly with **¾ cup shredded sharp Cheddar cheese;** broil about **3 MINUTES** or until cheese is bubbly.

PIZZA
Cups

Bite-size tortilla chip cups are filled with cheese, pesto, and tomatoes, then baked until bubbly.

PREP
20
min

SERVES
8

Preheat oven to 425°F. Place **40 bite-size tortilla chip cups** on large cookie sheet. In medium bowl, stir together **1 cup shredded Italian cheese blend** with **2 tablespoons store-bought pesto.** Spoon cheese mixture into chips. Slice **10 grape tomatoes** into 4 pieces each; place 1 on each pizza bite. Bake **6 MINUTES** or until cheese melts.

KITCHEN HACK

Can't find tortilla chip cups? Use an equal amount of regular chips. They're larger, so divide the chips between 2 cookie sheets.

Spicy
NACHOS

This recipe is so speedy, there's even time built-in to zap tortillas to make your own crispy chips.

PREP
15
min

SERVES
4

Preheat oven to 400°F. Place **1 corn tortilla** between 2 paper towels; microwave on High **1½ MINUTES** or until crisp. Repeat with **3 corn tortillas.** Break tortillas into large pieces; place in 8- by 8-inch glass baking dish. Top with **¾ cup canned refried beans, ½ cup shredded sharp Cheddar cheese,** and **1 tablespoon chopped pickled jalapeño chile.** Bake **8 MINUTES** or until cheese has melted. Top with **1 green onion,** sliced.

Jalapeño Bites

Honeyed
FIGS & BRIE

This elegant fall appetizer works beautifully with either extra-sweet black mission figs or nutty-tasting calimyrna figs.

PREP
15
min

SERVES
6

Arrange **4 ounces Brie cheese,** cut into small wedges, on large plate in single layer. Place **12 halved fresh figs,** cut sides up, on top. In small saucepan, bring ¼ **cup honey,** *1 tablespoon water,* and **4 sprigs fresh thyme** to boiling over medium-high heat, about **2 MINUTES.** Cook **1 MINUTE.** Drizzle honey mixture over figs; sprinkle with ¼ **teaspoon freshly ground black pepper.**

PUNCH IT UP!
Frozen Potato Pancakes

CINNAMON-APPLE LATKES

Top pancakes with **½ cup plain Greek yogurt** and **½ cup applesauce.** Sprinkle with **ground cinnamon.**

SMOKED SALMON LATKES

Use nondairy sour cream if you keep kosher.

Top pancakes with **½ cup sour cream; 8 ounces sliced smoked salmon; ¼ cup fresh dill sprigs;** and **¼ small red onion,** very thinly sliced.

---

*Tired of the same-old latkes? Cook 8 frozen potato pancakes as directed on label (the cooking time will be about **10 minutes**), then choose from these sensational 5-minute toppers. All recipes make 8 servings.*

STEAKHOUSE-STYLE LATKES

Mix **½ cup sour cream** and **1 tablespoon prepared horseradish,** drained; divide among pancakes. Top with **¼ pound deli-sliced roast beef** and **⅓ cup watercress leaves**.

BEET–BLUE CHEESE LATKES

Top pancakes with **½ cup sour cream; ½ (15-ounce) can sliced beets,** diced; **⅓ cup chopped walnuts,** toasted; and **¼ cup crumbled blue cheese.**

Cheddar-
Beer
Fondue

Cheddar-Beer FONDUE

Traditional fondue may be tasty, but if you want to feed a hungry crew, opt for this hearty dip with extra fixings. For more robust flavor, use dark beer.

PREP	MAKES
20	**2½**
min	*cups*

In large bowl, toss **1 package (16 ounces) shredded sharp Cheddar cheese** with **2 tablespoons cornstarch.** In 4-quart saucepan, combine **1 can (12 ounces) beer; 1 garlic clove,** crushed with press; **½ teaspoon Dijon mustard;** and **¼ teaspoon hot pepper sauce;** heat over medium heat **5 MINUTES** or until hot. Whisk in cheese mixture until melted and smooth. Serve with **sliced cooked sausage, cooked new potatoes, bread cubes,** and **apple slices** for dipping.

Holiday CHEESE BALL

This cheesy favorite with dried cranberry and pistachio coating can be stashed in the fridge up to 3 days, making it a perfect choice for an impromptu party.

PREP	SERVES
15	**8**
min	

In large bowl, with mixer at medium speed, beat **1 package (8 ounces) cream cheese,** softened; **1 package (8 ounces) shredded extra-sharp Cheddar cheese;** and ⅓ **cup sour cream** until smooth. Roll into ball, then roll in **¼ cup chopped pistachios** and **¼ cup dried cranberries.** Wrap in plastic wrap and refrigerate **1 HOUR** or until firm.

Bar
NUTS

Bacon adds a delectable smoky flavor to an otherwise ordinary bowl of peanuts. For a fancier snack, substitute cashews for half the amount of peanuts.

PREP
10
min

MAKES
2½
cups

In 12-inch skillet, cook **6 slices bacon,** chopped, over medium heat **8 MINUTES** or until browned. Drain off fat, reserving bacon in pan. Stir in **2 cups roasted, salted peanuts, 1 teaspoon sugar,** and **½ teaspoon ground red pepper (cayenne).** Cook, stirring frequently, **2 MINUTES** or until nuts are lightly browned. Transfer to large plate and cool completely.

KITCHEN HACK Instead of chopping the bacon, snip the slices with kitchen shears straight into the skillet.

Spiced
MUNCHIES

These distinctively different bites start with a (surprise!) can of chickpeas.

PREP
10
min

MAKES
1¼
cups

Preheat oven to 425°F. In 15½- by 10½-inch jelly-roll pan, toss **1 can (15 ounces) chickpeas,** rinsed and drained well, with **2 tablespoons vegetable oil; 1 teaspoon ground coriander; ¼ teaspoon ground red pepper (cayenne);** and **¼ teaspoon salt;** then coat with **1 tablespoon flour.** Spread in an even layer. Roast, stirring once, about **25 MINUTES** or until golden and crisp. Cool on paper towels.

Spiced Munchies

Speedy
SOUPS
&
SALADS

You'll have plenty of time to mix 'em,
match 'em, or savor 'em solo.

BUTTERNUT SQUASH

Soup

Applesauce adds an unexpected note of sweetness to this silky smooth soup.

PREP
20
min

SERVES
4

In 3-quart saucepan, melt **1 tablespoon butter or margarine** over medium-high heat. Stir in **1 teaspoon ground ginger**. Add **1 package (20 ounces) peeled, cubed butternut squash** and *3 cups water*. Heat to boiling over high heat, about **10 MINUTES**. Reduce heat to medium; cook **15 MINUTES** or until squash is tender. Stir in **1½ cups unsweetened applesauce;** cook **1 MINUTE**. Puree in batches in blender (with center part of cover removed to let steam escape) until smooth. Stir in **1 tablespoon butter or margarine, ½ teaspoon salt,** and **¼ teaspoon freshly ground black pepper.** Divide among 4 bowls; sprinkle with **croutons** and **fresh sage leaves.**

KITCHEN HACK

Look for convenient peeled, cubed butternut squash in the produce section at the supermarket.

Creamy AVOCADO SOUP

Jarred salsa verde does double-duty in this refreshing soup: It delivers zesty flavor while keeping the avocado bright green.

PREP
15
min

SERVES
4

In blender, puree **1 ripe avocado,** pitted and peeled; **1 cup sour cream;** *1 cup cold water;* **¾ cup salsa verde; ¼ cup packed fresh cilantro leaves; ½ teaspoon salt;** and **½ teaspoon freshly ground black pepper** until smooth. Cover and refrigerate until cold, at least **2 HOURS**. Divide among 4 bowls; sprinkle with **roasted, salted pumpkin seeds** and **fresh cilantro leaves.**

KITCHEN HACK

Prep an avocado in seconds! Cut it lengthwise into quarters, working around the pit; separate the 4 sections. With thumb and index finger, remove the pit. Slide your thumb under the skin of each section and peel the skin back.

89

Easy
MINESTRONE

Traditional minestrone is often labor intensive—not so with a bag of frozen Italian veggies.

PREP
15
min

SERVES
4

In 4-quart saucepan, combine **1 can (15 or 19 ounces) red kidney beans,** rinsed and drained well; **1 carton (32 ounces) chicken or vegetable broth; 1 can (14½ ounces) diced tomatoes with onion and garlic;** and **¼ teaspoon Italian seasoning;** cover and heat over high heat to boiling, about **10 MINUTES.** Stir in **1 bag (16 ounces) frozen Italian vegetables;** cover and cook **6 MINUTES** or until tender. Serve with **freshly grated Parmesan cheese.**

DINNER IN A DASH
Try these soup and salad combos!

COMBO ONE
Creamy Avocado Soup (p. 89)
Red, White & Green Salad (p. 98)

COMBO TWO
Easy Minestrone (p. 90)
Hearty Ham Salad (p. 97)

COMBO THREE
Butternut Squash Soup (p. 86)
Pineapple-Bacon Salad (p. 123)

BROCCOLI-CHEDDAR
Soup

A bag of frozen broccoli keeps this cheesy favorite simple.

PREP
15
min

SERVES
4

In 4-quart saucepan, heat **1¾ cups chicken broth; 1 medium potato,** peeled and chopped; and **¼ teaspoon** salt to boiling over high heat, about **5 MINUTES**. Chop **1 bag (16 ounces) frozen broccoli,** thawed; add half to pot. Reduce heat to medium; cook **10 MINUTES** or until potato is tender. Puree in blender in batches (with center part of cover removed to let steam escape) until smooth. Return to pan; add remaining broccoli, **1 cup milk,** and **1 package (8 ounces) shredded Cheddar cheese.** Cook, stirring, over medium heat **5 MINUTES** or until cheese melts.

Chilled
BEET-CARROT SOUP

In blender, puree **1 package (8 to 9 ounces) whole, unseasoned, precooked peeled red beets, 1½ cups carrot juice, ½ teaspoon finely grated lemon peel, 2 tablespoons fresh lemon juice, ¼ cup sour cream,** and **½ teaspoon salt** until very smooth. Cover and refrigerate until cold, at least **2 HOURS**. Divide among 4 bowls; top evenly with **4 teaspoons sour cream** and **fresh dill sprigs**.

KITCHEN HACK

Thick-skinned lemons with pebbly (versus smooth) peels are the easiest to grate.

Love beets, but hate to cook and peel them? This quickie soup is a whizz away with precooked beets and fresh carrot juice.

PREP
15
min

SERVES
4

Classic
VINAIGRETTE

If a great salad is judged by its dressing, this is your go-to recipe to impress. Cover and refrigerate any extras up to 3 days.

PREP
5
min

SERVES
6

¼ cup red wine vinegar
1 tablespoon Dijon mustard
¼ teaspoon salt
¼ teaspoon freshly ground black pepper
½ cup extra-virgin olive oil

In medium bowl, with wire whisk, stir together vinegar, mustard, salt, and pepper. Continue whisking and add oil in a slow, steady stream. Whisk until well blended and emulsified.

Our Classic Vinaigrette can be tossed with everything from greens to grains. It's also a snap to swap in ingredients for a trio of tasty dressings below. All recipes make ¾ cup or enough for 6 servings.

BALSAMIC VINAIGRETTE

Prepare vinaigrette as directed but substitute **balsamic vinegar** for red wine vinegar.

LEMON VINAIGRETTE

Prepare vinaigrette as directed but substitute **fresh lemon juice** for red wine vinegar.

HERB VINAIGRETTE

Prepare vinaigrette as directed but substitute **white wine vinegar** for red wine vinegar. Stir in **1 tablespoon chopped fresh chives** and **1 teaspoon chopped fresh tarragon.**

Hearty
HAM
SALAD

Conveniently packaged hearts of romaine are not only crispier than the darker outer lettuce leaves, they taste sweeter too.

PREP
10
min

SERVES
4

In large bowl, toss **1 can (15 ounces) pink beans,** rinsed and drained well; **2 hearts romaine lettuce,** chopped; **2 stalks celery,** sliced; **½ cup diced smoked ham;** and ¼ **cup Balsamic Vinaigrette** (p. 95).

KITCHEN HACK

Upgrade your salad by swapping ½ small trimmed and sliced fennel bulb for the celery.

97

RED, WHITE & GREEN *Salad*

Sweet strawberries have a natural flavor affinity with balsamic vinegar, so we paired that dynamic duo to dress leafy green salad with chicken and goat cheese.

PREP
15
min

SERVES
4

In large bowl, combine **1 pound strawberries,** hulled and sliced; **2 tablespoons balsamic vinegar; ¼ teaspoon salt;** and **¼ teaspoon freshly ground black pepper.** Let stand **10 MINUTES,** stirring often. Add **1 package (5 ounces) baby greens and herbs mix** and **3 cups coarsely shredded cooked chicken;** toss to combine. Divide among 4 plates. Top evenly with **4 ounces herbed goat cheese,** crumbled.

KITCHEN HACK

Use white meat from a rotisserie chicken.

SHRIMP
& Green Apple
SALAD

While Granny Smith apples are readily available year round, if it's fall, try this salad with a tart green apple like Newton Pippin if it's available at your farmers' market.

PREP
10
min

SERVES
2

Toss **12 ounces cooked, shelled, and deveined shrimp; 1 small Granny Smith apple,** thinly sliced; **½ seedless (English) cucumber,** thinly sliced; **3 tablespoons orange juice; 2 tablespoons extra-virgin olive oil;** and **1 teaspoon hot pepper sauce;** arrange on two dinner plates. Sprinkle with **¼ teaspoon salt, ¼ teaspoon freshly ground black pepper,** and **2 tablespoons pine nuts,** toasted.

KITCHEN
HACK

To toast the pine nuts, place them in a small dry skillet and cook, stirring frequently, 3 minutes or until golden in spots.

Smoky CORN SALAD

Fresh corn kernels are charred in a hot skillet then tossed with a spicy lime dressing.

PREP
15
min

SERVES
4

Heat 12-inch cast-iron or other heavy skillet over medium-high until hot. Add **2 cups fresh corn kernels** and cook, stirring occasionally, **3 MINUTES** or until browned. Transfer to large bowl and immediately stir in **2 tablespoons fresh lime juice** and **1/8 teaspoon chipotle chile powder.** Cool slightly, then stir in **1 cup finely chopped red pepper, 1/2 cup fresh cilantro leaves,** and **1/8 teaspoon salt.**

BARLEY-CHERRY Salad

For the perfect summer supper, pair this fruity grain salad with store-bought rotisserie chicken.

PREP
15
min

SERVES
6

In covered 2-quart saucepan, heat *2 cups water* over high heat to boiling, **3 TO 5 MINUTES**. Stir in **1 cup pearl barley** and **1/2 teaspoon salt;** heat to boiling. Reduce heat to low; cover and simmer **30 TO 35 MINUTES** or until barley is tender. Drain in colander, rinse until cool, and drain again. Meanwhile, pit and chop **12 ounces fresh cherries**, thinly slice **3 stalks celery,** and chop **1/4 cup fresh mint leaves.** In large bowl, toss barley, cherries, celery, mint, **2 tablespoons cider vinegar,** and **1/2 teaspoon salt** until mixed.

KITCHEN HACK

Toast the barley before cooking to bring out its nutty flavor. Heat I teaspoon olive oil in the saucepan over medium-high heat. Add the barley; cook, stirring constantly, 3 minutes or until fragrant, then add the water.

Barley-Cherry Salad

KALE

It's a fabulous pick for hearty soups and salads.

WHAT'S YOUR KALE IQ?

Fact: This trendy green veggie is actually a member of the cabbage family—the caveat being the central leaves don't form a head. You also have three varieties to choose from (details right). Best of all, whether you enjoy kale in a soup or salad, all varieties can be used interchangeably.

CURLY KALE Ruffled, firm leaves that range from green to almost blue-green; mild, slightly sweet.

DINOSAUR (LACINATO) KALE Flat, narrow, deep green leaves, with a pebbled texture; more tender than curly kale; pungent with a hint of spiciness.

RED RUSSIAN KALE Lacy, silver-green leaves with red stalks and purple veins; sweet and tender.

KALE & WHITE BEAN Soup

Looking for a warming meal? This hearty soup is a perfect way to enjoy curly kale, which is at its sweetest in the winter months.

PREP
20
min

SERVES
4

Cut **2 fully cooked chorizo sausages (2½ ounces)** into ¼-inch pieces. In 7-quart saucepot, cook chorizo, stirring occasionally, over medium heat **3 MINUTES** or until browned and crisp. Stir in **1 large onion,** chopped; cook **5 MINUTES** or until tender. Stir in **10 cups chopped kale leaves** (from 1 small bunch) and **¼ teaspoon freshly ground black pepper;** cook **1 MINUTE**. Add **1 can (14½ ounces) stewed tomatoes** with their juices, crushed; **1 can (15 to 15½ ounces) white beans,** rinsed and drained; and *2 cups water*. Heat over high heat to boiling, about **10 MINUTES**. Reduce heat to medium-low and simmer **10 MINUTES** or until kale is tender. Stir in **¼ teaspoon salt.**

KITCHEN HACK

Save on knife work and use a 10-ounce bag of ready-to-use chopped fresh kale.

KALE Slaw

This trendy take on coleslaw is excellent with dinosaur (Lacinato) kale.

PREP
15
min

SERVES
4

In large bowl, whisk together **3 tablespoons fresh lemon juice, 2 tablespoons mayonnaise, 2 tablespoons olive oil, 1 tablespoon Dijon mustard, ⅛ teaspoon salt,** and **⅛ teaspoon freshly ground black pepper.** Add **3 cups thinly sliced kale; 1 small apple,** chopped; and **½ cup walnuts,** toasted and chopped; toss to combine.

Wilted KALE SALAD

Sturdy kale leaves make an ideal alternative to spinach because they hold their shape when tossed with hot dressings.

PREP
15
min

SERVES
4

In 12-inch skillet, cook **6 slices bacon,** chopped, over medium heat, stirring occasionally, **8 MINUTES** or until crisp. Stir in **1 cup chopped onion;** cook **8 MINUTES** or until tender. Meanwhile, in large bowl, whisk together **2 tablespoons red wine vinegar, ¼ teaspoon salt,** and **¼ teaspoon freshly ground black pepper.** Add **7 cups thinly sliced kale leaves** and toss to coat. Add bacon mixture and toss again. Top with **½ cup crumbled goat cheese.**

Lemony KALE SALAD

What's the secret to a great kale salad? Let the greens stand in the dressing 5 minutes. That will mellow the pungent taste and soften its slightly chewy texture.

PREP
15
min

SERVES
4

In large bowl, whisk together **2 tablespoons fresh lemon juice, 2 tablespoons extra-virgin olive oil,** and **⅛ teaspoon salt;** add **6 cups thinly sliced kale;** toss to coat. Let stand 5 minutes. Add **½ cup pitted dates,** cut into slivers; **⅓ cup roasted salted almonds,** chopped; and **¼ cup jarred pitted green olives,** sliced; toss to combine.

KITCHEN HACK

To get the kale salad-ready, strip the leaves of their tough stems with your hands. Then stack a few leaves at a time on a cutting board and roll them into a cigar-shape Use a sharp knife to cut into thin ribbons.

Lemony Kale Sald

ICEBERG WEDGES

WITH

Tangy Russian Dressing

Make a double batch of dressing and use the extra for an instant chicken or seafood salad. It will keep in the fridge up to 1 week.

PREP
10
min

SERVES
4

In medium bowl, whisk together **½ cup mayonnaise, ¼ cup ketchup, 2 tablespoons sweet pickle relish, 1 tablespoon fresh lemon juice, ¼ teaspoon salt,** and **¼ teaspoon freshly ground black pepper.** Spoon over **1 head iceberg lettuce,** cut into 4 wedges.

KITCHEN HACK

To wash iceberg lettuce, remove the core with a paring knife. Rinse the head, cored-side up, under cold running water. Turn the head over and shake it to remove any excess water. Drain on a clean kitchen towel or in a colander.

109

ALPHABET
Soup

Garnish each serving of soup with a teaspoon of store-bought pesto.

PREP
10
min

SERVES
6

In 5-quart saucepan, combine **1 carton (32 ounces) chicken broth, 4 cups tomato-vegetable juice, 1 package (16 ounces) frozen mixed vegetables, ½ teaspoon Italian seasoning,** and **¼ teaspoon freshly ground black pepper.** Cover and heat to boiling over high heat, about **10 MINUTES**. Stir in **1 cup uncooked alphabet pasta or orzo.** Reduce heat to medium-low and simmer, uncovered, **8 MINUTES** or until pasta and vegetables are tender.

POTATO
&
"LEEK"
Soup

Instead of using leeks, which can be gritty and time-consuming to clean, we swapped in easy-to-prep green onions. The result: Sensational flavor in a fraction of the time.

PREP
15
min

SERVES
4

In 3-quart saucepan, melt **1 tablespoon butter or margarine** over medium heat. Add **2 bunches green onions,** sliced, and cook, stirring frequently, **2 MINUTES** or until softened. Add **1 carton (32 ounces) chicken broth, 1 cup milk,** and **¼ teaspoon freshly ground black pepper;** heat to boiling over high heat, about **10 MINUTES**. Stir in **1¼ cups instant mashed potato flakes.** Puree in batches in blender, with center part of cover removed to let steam escape, until smooth. Divide among 4 bowls; sprinkle with **fresh dill sprigs.**

Potato & "Leek" Soup

French Potato Salad

French POTATO SALAD

No need to peel thin-skinned Yukon Gold potatoes for this classic warm salad.

PREP **20** *min* | SERVES **4**

In 5-quart saucepot, place **2 pounds Yukon Gold potatoes,** cut into 1-inch chunks; enough *cold water* to cover; and **1 teaspoon salt;** heat to boiling over high heat, **10 TO 15 MINUTES**. Reduce heat; cover and simmer **12 TO 13 MINUTES** or until tender. Meanwhile, in large bowl, whisk together **3 tablespoons white wine vinegar, 2 tablespoons snipped fresh chives, 1 tablespoon extra-virgin olive oil, 1 teaspoon Dijon mustard, ¼ teaspoon salt,** and **⅛ teaspoon freshly ground black pepper.** Drain potatoes. Add hot potatoes to dressing in bowl; gently toss until well mixed. Serve warm.

Creamy ARTICHOKE-PARMESAN Soup

Select canned artichoke hearts packed in brine (versus marinated) and rinse well before using.

PREP **20** *min* | SERVES **4**

In 5-quart saucepan, combine **2 teaspoons extra-virgin olive oil** and **2 shallots,** sliced. Cook over medium-low heat **5 MINUTES** or until golden. Add **1 can (13¾ to 14 ounces) artichoke hearts in brine,** rinsed and drained, and **1 small potato,** peeled and chopped. Increase heat to medium-high and cook, stirring, **2 MINUTES**. Add *4 cups water;* heat to boiling, about **10 MINUTES**. Reduce heat; simmer **15 TO 20 MINUTES** or until potato is tender. Stir in **¼ teaspoon salt** and **pinch freshly ground black pepper.** Puree in batches in blender, with center part of cover removed to let steam escape, until smooth. Divide among 4 bowls. Garnish with **shaved Parmesan cheese;** drizzle with **extra-virgin olive oil.**

Winter SLAW

Using a food processor with a shredding blade makes quick work of this salad. You'll need 2 pounds of celery root and 3 carrots for the recipe.

PREP
15
min

SERVES
6

In large bowl, whisk together **⅓ cup mayonnaise, 2 tablespoons fresh lemon juice, 2 tablespoons extra-virgin olive oil, 1 tablespoon Dijon mustard, ½ teaspoon salt,** and **¼ teaspoon freshly ground black pepper.** Add **6 cups shredded, peeled celery root, 1 cup shredded carrots,** and **¼ cup sliced fresh flat-leaf parsley.** Toss until well coated.

ROOT JOB

With its clod-like shape and gnarly tendrils, celery root looks downright frightening. But give this veg a serious facial and you're in for a big secret: luxurious texture and taste. If you can find super-fresh celery root with its stalks, trim and refrigerate separately to perfume soups and stews; remove prior to serving (use sparingly as they are more potent than celery).

SELECT While tangled roots are okay, look for smoothish-skinned bulbs (they'll be easier to peel). Press the stalk end of the bulb, opposite the roots. It should be firm, not spongy.

PREP Scrub with a brush to remove excess grit. Trim and discard top and bottom of bulb. Cut into quarters, trim any spongy portion from center, then peel with a knife.

STORE Chill in plastic bag up to 2 weeks.

COOL-AS-A-CUKE BUTTERMILK SOUP

Look for super-fresh English cukes (minus their plastic shrink wrap) at the farmers' market. Or try similar Persian cucumbers if available.

In blender, puree 2 peeled and chopped cucumbers, **1 cup buttermilk, ¼ cup fresh mint leaves, ½ teaspoon salt,** and **¼ teaspoon freshly ground black pepper.** Stir in **1 cup buttermilk.** Cover and refrigerate until cold, at least **2 HOURS.** Garnish with **snipped fresh chives.**

Who knew this queen of cucumbers was so user-friendly? Sweet and crisp, English cukes aren't waxed, so there's no need to peel them. Plus, they're virtually seedless, so you can skip that step too. You'll need one to two 13- to 14-ounce cukes for these 20-minute dishes. All recipes make 4 servings.

MEDITERRANEAN TUNA

In bowl, mix 1 cucumber, cut into ¾-inch chunks; **2 cans (5 ounces each) drained and flaked tuna; ⅓ cup pitted and chopped Kalamata olives; 2 small chopped tomatoes;** and **3 tablespoons Lemon Vinaigrette (page 95).** Serve over **mesclun.**

SCANDINAVIAN SHRIMP SALAD

In bowl, mix 1 very thinly sliced cucumber, **1 pound shelled and deveined cooked shrimp, ½ cup sour cream, 2 tablespoons chopped fresh dill, ¼ teaspoon finely grated lemon peel, 2 tablespoons fresh lemon juice, ¼ teaspoon salt,** and **⅛ teaspoon freshly ground black pepper.**

Peppers
CAPRESE

Select red, orange, or yellow peppers for this dish; they're sweeter than the green variety.

PREP
15
min

SERVES
4

In large bowl, whisk together **2 tablespoons red wine vinegar, 2 tablespoons extra-virgin olive oil, ½ teaspoon salt,** and **¼ teaspoon freshly ground black pepper.** Add **3 medium peppers,** cut into thin slices. Toss until well coated. Let stand **10 MINUTES**. Meanwhile, thinly slice **⅓ cup fresh basil leaves** and cut **4 ounces bocconcini (small mozzarella balls)** into 1-inch pieces. Toss basil and bocconcini with peppers.

THREE-
BEAN
Salad

For a Tex-Mex twist, swap in black beans for the pink, lime juice for the vinegar, and cilantro for the tarragon.

Heat 3-quart saucepan of salted water over high heat to boiling, about **10 MINUTES**. Add **8 ounces wax or green beans,** trimmed and cut into 2-inch pieces. Cook **4 MINUTES** or until crisp-tender. Add **8 ounces frozen edamame** to beans; cook **2 MINUTES**. Drain beans and edamame in colander. Rinse under cold water until cool; drain again. Meanwhile, in large bowl, whisk together **2 tablespoons white wine vinegar, 1 tablespoon extra-virgin olive oil, 1/4 teaspoon salt,** and **1/4 teaspoon freshly ground black pepper.** Add **1 can (15 to 15 1/2 ounces) pink beans,** rinsed and drained well. Stir in wax beans and edamame and **2 tablespoons chopped fresh tarragon.**

PREP
20
min

SERVES
4

KITCHEN
HACK

To save time, just trim the stems of the wax or green beans; the pretty tail ends are completely edible.

CANTALOUPE GOAT CHEESE *Salad*

This summery salad also works beautifully with honeydew melon.

PREP
15
min

SERVES
4

Remove peel and seeds from **1 small cantaloupe;** discard. Cut melon into 1-inch chunks. Arrange on large plate. Drizzle **1 tablespoon fresh lime or lemon juice** and **1 tablespoon extra-virgin olive oil** over melon, then sprinkle with **⅛ teaspoon chipotle chile powder, teaspoon salt.** Scatter **2 ounces goat cheese,** crumbled, and **2 tablespoons fresh mint leaves,** torn, over melon.

CARROT & ZUCCHINI *Ribbon Salad*

A dash of chipotle chile powder lends smoky heat to this salad. But if you prefer a milder version, it's equally tasty with smoked paprika.

PREP
20
min

SERVES
4

In large bowl, whisk together **1 tablespoon fresh lime juice, 1 teaspoon vegetable oil, ¼ teaspoon salt, ¼ teaspoon freshly ground black pepper,** and **⅛ teaspoon chipotle chile powder.** Peel **3 medium carrots,** then use vegetable peeler to form long ribbons. Stop peeling when you reach core; discard. Shave **1 large zucchini** into ribbons; stop peeling when you reach seeds; discard. Cut all ribbons in half. Add carrot ribbons, zucchini ribbons, and **¼ cup fresh cilantro leaves** to bowl with dressing; toss until evenly coated.

Carrot & Zucchini Ribbon Salad

Watermelon-Arugula Salad

WATERMELON-ARUGULA Salad

Super-sweet watermelon and pecans are a perfect match for extra-peppery arugula.

PREP
15
min

SERVES
4

In large bowl, whisk together **2 tablespoons extra-virgin olive oil, 2 tablespoons red wine vinegar, and ¼ teaspoon salt.** Add **3 cups cubed seedless watermelon; 3 cups sliced peaches; 3 cups baby arugula; ½ cup packed fresh basil leaves;** and **¼ cup hazelnuts,** toasted and chopped.

KITCHEN HACK

Look for blanched hazelnuts, sold without their pesky skins, in specialty food markets. To toast, bake the nuts in a toaster oven at 350°F 8 to 10 minutes or until golden and fragrant.

PINEAPPLE-BACON Salad

There's a double dose of juicy sweet pineapple in this refreshing green salad.

PREP
15
min

SERVES
6

In blender, puree **½ cup chopped fresh pineapple, 2 tablespoons champagne vinegar, ⅛ teaspoon chipotle chile powder, teaspoon crushed red pepper, ¼ teaspoon salt,** and **¼ teaspoon freshly ground black pepper** until smooth. With blender running and center part of cover removed, drizzle in **¼ cup extra-virgin olive oil.** Transfer dressing to large bowl. Add **2 cups chopped fresh pineapple; 1 package (5 ounces) baby arugula;** and **2 romaine lettuce hearts,** chopped; toss to coat. Top with **6 slices cooked bacon,** crumbled.

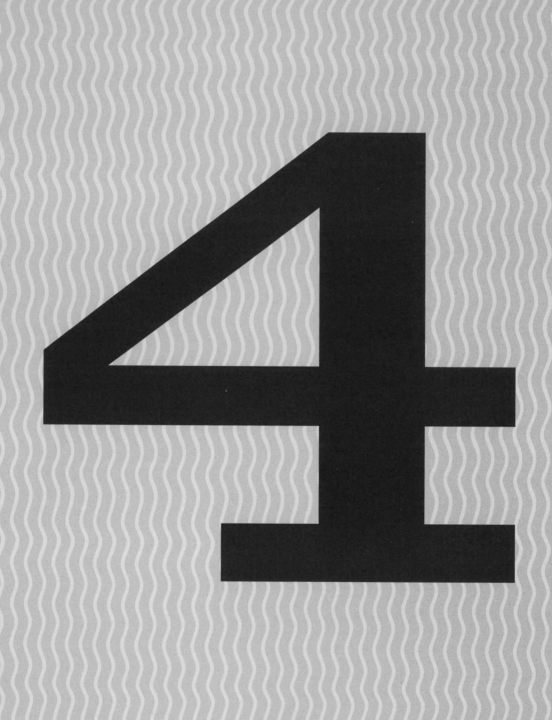

Master Your
MAINS

Lunch and dinner are now
ready in no time.

PUNCH IT UP!
"Haute" Dogs

PIMIENTO-CHEESE DOGS

In medium bowl, combine **1½ cups shredded Cheddar cheese**, **¼ cup minced jarred pimientos**, **¼ cup mayonnaise**, and **½ teaspoon hot sauce**; divide among 4 hot dogs.

············

EVERYTHING BAGEL DOGS

In small bowl, beat **3 tablespoons softened cream cheese, 2 tablespoons milk,** and **¼ teaspoon salt** until smooth. Divide among 4 hot dogs; sprinkle with **1 teaspoon poppy seeds** and **2 sliced green onions.**

Hold the mustard! These 5-minute toppers pack some serious pizzazz. All recipes make 4 servings.

BLT DOGS

Divide **¼ cup mayonnaise, ½ cup sliced romaine lettuce, 1 chopped tomato,** and **6 slices cooked crumbled bacon** among 4 hot dogs.

············

SPICY BLUE CHEESE DOGS

In medium bowl, combine **1 cup chopped celery, ¼ cup mayonnaise, ½ teaspoon cider vinegar, ½ teaspoon hot sauce,** and **¾ cup crumbled blue cheese;** divide among 4 hot dogs.

KITCHEN HACK

Don't pierce hot dogs with a fork when cooking. The juices will run out, resulting in a tough and dry dog.

Pimiento-Cheese Dogs

Everything Bagel Dogs

BLT Dogs

Spicy Blue Cheese Dogs

The ULTIMATE BURGER

Welcome to burger nirvana! This recipe also works beautifully with ground lamb, pork, or turkey.

PREP
10
min

SERVES
4

1¼ **pounds 85% lean ground beef**
½ **teaspoon kosher salt**
¼ **teaspoon freshly ground black pepper**
4 **hamburger buns, toasted**

1. Divide beef into 4 mounds (about 5 ounces each) and loosely shape into balls. Using your hands, gently flatten balls into four ¾-inch-thick burgers. Smooth burger edges with your fingers.

2. Place burgers on flat surface. Using your thumbs, press in centers of burgers to make deep indentations. Refrigerate until ready to grill.

3. Prepare outdoor grill for direct grilling over medium-high heat. Sprinkle burgers with salt and pepper. Place burgers on grill. Cook, turning once, **7 MINUTES** for medium-well or until desired doneness. (Instant-read thermometer inserted horizontally into center of burger should reach 160°F.) Serve on buns.

BUILD A DISH

*Here's something to flip for: Fire up our Ultimate Burger, then add
a 5-minute gourmet topping. All recipes make 4 servings.*

TAPAS BURGER

In mini food processor, puree **½ cup roasted red peppers,** drained and patted dry, and **¼ cup mayonnaise** until smooth. Divide **½ cup grated Manchego cheese** and pepper mixture among burgers.

ISLAND BURGER

Divide **½ cup shredded pepper Jack cheese, 1 thinly sliced green onion,** and **4 fresh pineapple rings** among burgers.

HOT HOISIN BURGERS

In small bowl, stir together **2½ tablespoons hoisin sauce** and **1½ tablespoons sriracha.** Divide among burgers. Top with **fresh cilantro leaves.**

THE SO. CAL BURGER

In small bowl, mash together **1 pitted and peeled ripe avocado; 2 tablespoons mayonnaise;** and **½ clove garlic,** crushed with press. Divide among burgers. Top with **shredded carrots** and **alfalfa sprouts.**

HAMBURGER 101

While grilling a burger packed with big beefy flavor and dripping juice isn't rocket science, there are a few simple tricks to follow.

"MEAT" THE BUTCHER and order freshly ground chuck. It's guaranteed to beat the stuff that's been sitting in a Styrofoam tray for days.

GENTLY HANDLE the meat when shaping into patties; overworking will make it tough.

MAKE THUMBPRINTS in the center of each patty. Burgers contract as they cook, causing the middle to push up into a dome. Indentations solve that problem so the burgers cook evenly.

SPATULAS ARE FOR FLIPPING, not pressing. All you'll accomplish is to push the juice out of the burger.

STEAK

WITH
Green Sauce

Lightly spray **2 boneless beef top loin steaks,** each 1 inch thick (2 pounds total), with nonstick cooking spray; sprinkle with **¼ teaspoon salt** and **¼ teaspoon freshly ground black pepper.** Heat grill pan over medium-high heat until hot. Add steaks; cook, turning once, **8 TO 10 MINUTES** for medium-rare or until desired doneness. Transfer to cutting board. In small bowl, whisk together **2 cups fresh flat-leaf parsley,** chopped; **⅓ cup cornichons,** chopped, plus 3 tablespoons of their juice; **¼ cup extra-virgin olive oil;** and *1 tablespoon water.* Serve steaks with sauce.

Cornichons, tiny little pickles from France, lend a piquant flavor to the speedy parsley sauce.

KITCHEN HACK

Don't waste time poking a steak to check for doneness. An instant-read thermometer will give you the info in seconds. Insert the stem horizontally into the center of each steak; it should reach 140°F for medium-rare.

PREP
15
min

SERVES
4

STEAK
WITH
Red Wine

Turn leftover red wine into a fabulous steak dinner for company.

PREP
10
min

SERVES
4

Sprinkle **1 beef flank steak** (1 pound) with **½ teaspoon salt** and **¼ teaspoon freshly ground pepper.** In 12-inch skillet, heat **1 tablespoon olive oil** over medium-high heat. Add steak; cook, turning once, **12 TO 14 MINUTES** for medium-rare or until desired doneness. Transfer to cutting board. To skillet, add **2 teaspoons fresh thyme leaves** and **1 cup red wine.** Cook **3 TO 5 MINUTES** or until reduced by half. Remove from heat; whisk in **¼ cup heavy or whipping cream** and **⅛ teaspoon salt.** Serve over steak.

Adobo
STEAK

Canned chipotles en adobo (aka dried smoked jalapeño chiles in a tangy, slightly sweet sauce) give these steaks their fiery punch.

PREP
10
min

SERVES
4

In small bowl, mix **⅔ cup sour cream, 1 tablespoon fresh lime juice, 2 teaspoons finely chopped chipotle chile in adobo, ¼ teaspoon ground cumin,** and **¼ teaspoon salt.** In large bowl, mix **2 tablespoons adobo sauce, 1 teaspoon ground cumin, ¼ teaspoon salt,** and **¼ teaspoon freshly ground black pepper;** add **4 boneless top loin beef steaks,** each ½ inch thick (2 pounds total); toss to coat. Let stand **10 MINUTES.** Meanwhile, prepare outdoor grill for direct grilling over medium-high heat. Place steaks on grill. Cook, turning once, **7 TO 8 MINUTES** for medium-rare or until desired doneness. Serve with chipotle cream.

ASPARAGUS

This best-of-spring veggie adds instant elegance to any dish.

STALKING DELICIOUS

Delectable asparagus starts with these shopping smarts.

CHOOSE firm, bright-green asparagus with plump, tightly closed tips. The stem ends should look freshly cut, not shriveled or dried out.

OPT for bunches with similar-sized spears so they'll cook at the same rate.

ENJOY asparagus the day you buy it. Or, wrap the stem ends in a damp paper towel, place in a plastic bag, and refrigerate up to 4 days.

KITCHEN HACK

To speed-trim asparagus, keep the band or ties around the bunch, then cut off the white stem ends with a large knife.

SALMON & ASPARAGUS Pasta

Thanks to pencil-thin asparagus and canned salmon, this lemony pasta is super-quick.

PREP
15
min

SERVES
4

Cook **12 ounces penne pasta** in *boiling salted water* 3 MINUTES less than package label directs, **6 TO 8 MINUTES**. Add **1 pound thin asparagus,** trimmed and cut into 1-inch pieces; cook **3 MINUTES**. Meanwhile, in 12-inch skillet, heat **2 tablespoons olive oil** over medium heat. Add **1 small onion,** chopped; cook **8 MINUTES** or until tender. Reserve *¼ cup pasta cooking water*. Drain penne and asparagus; return to pot and stir in **1 can (14¾ ounces) pink salmon,** drained well, skin and bones discarded, and flesh broken into bite-size pieces; onion; **1 teaspoon finely grated lemon peel; 2 tablespoons fresh lemon juice; ¼ teaspoon salt;** and **⅛ teaspoon freshly ground black pepper.** Stir in reserved cooking water.

Asparagus "RISOTTO"

Think risotto needs constant stirring? Not when you start with a package of rice pilaf mix.

PREP
10
min

SERVES
4

Cook **1 box (6- to 7-ounces) rice pilaf mix** as package label directs, about **25 MINUTES**. Stir in **1 pound thin asparagus**, trimmed and cut into 1-inch pieces, and **¾ cup reduced-sodium chicken broth;** cover and heat to boiling, about **2 MINUTES**. Reduce heat to low and simmer, covered, stirring occasionally, **3 TO 4 MINUTES** or until asparagus is crisp-tender. Remove from heat; add **2 ounces goat cheese,** crumbled; **1 teaspoon finely grated lemon peel;** and **1 tablespoon fresh lemon juice;** stir until cheese melts.

ASPARAGUS RICOTTA
Tart

Fact: The greener the asparagus, the tenderer it will be—and this skillet wonder is the perfect way to show it off.

PREP
10
min

SERVES
4

Preheat oven to 375°F. In large bowl, whisk together **1 container (15 ounces) ricotta cheese, 4 large eggs, ¼ cup freshly grated Parmesan cheese, ¼ cup milk, 3 tablespoons snipped fresh chives, ¼ teaspoon salt,** and **¼ teaspoon freshly ground black pepper.** Pour egg mixture into 10-inch nonstick oven-safe skillet; top with **8 ounces thin asparagus,** trimmed to fit. Bake **40 MINUTES** or until set.

Quick
CHICKEN KEBOBS

Zap a package of heat-and-serve precooked rice to serve alongside these summery kebobs with nectarines and green onion.

PREP
20
min

SERVES
4

Prepare outdoor grill for direct grilling over medium-high heat. In medium bowl, toss **1 pound skinless, boneless chicken thighs,** cubed; **3 tablespoons olive oil;** and **2 tablespoons soy sauce** until well coated. Thread chicken; **3 large nectarines,** cubed; and **1 bunch green onions,** cut into 1-inch pieces; alternately on 8 (12-inch) metal skewers. Place kebobs on grill; cook, turning once and basting with **¼ cup cider vinegar, 10 MINUTES** or until chicken is cooked through (165°F).

KITCHEN HACK

If using wooden skewers, soak them in water to cover at least 15 minutes, then drain. (That way they won't burn.)

CHICKEN- SAUSAGE
Stew

Hearty chicken thighs, smoky sausage, and apple cider make this skillet dinner taste like it's simmered for hours.

PREP
10
min

SERVES
4

In 12-inch nonstick skillet, heat **1 teaspoon olive oil** over medium-high heat. Sprinkle **1 pound skinless, boneless chicken thighs** with **¼ teaspoon salt** and **¼ teaspoon freshly ground black pepper.** Add to skillet along with **4 ounces turkey kielbasa,** chopped. Cook, turning, **5 MINUTES** or until browned. Add **4 celery stalks,** sliced, and **⅛ teaspoon salt.** Cook, stirring, **2 MINUTES**. Add **2 cups apple cider** and **1 tablespoon tomato paste.** Reduce heat to medium; simmer, stirring occasionally, **15 MINUTES** or until chicken is cooked through.

Honey-Mustard
CHICKEN FINGERS

Crushed cornflakes in the coating guarantee extra-crunchy chicken strips.

PREP
15
min

SERVES
4

Preheat oven to 450°F. Place wire rack in large jelly-roll pan. In pie plate, stir together **3 cups crushed cornflakes, 1 tablespoon honey, ½ teaspoon finely grated lemon peel, ½ teaspoon salt, and ¼ teaspoon freshly ground black pepper.** In large bowl, combine **1 pound chicken tenders** and **1 tablespoon Dijon mustard;** toss to coat. Dredge each piece chicken in cornflake mixture. Place on rack; bake **12 MINUTES** or until no longer pink in center.

KITCHEN HACK

Don't have a pie plate for the coating? Use a large sheet of wax paper.

Herbed
SKILLET
CHICKEN

We keep it quick and simple by combining all the ingredients right in the pan.

PREP
20
min

SERVES
4

Preheat oven to 450°F. In 12-inch cast-iron or other heavy skillet, toss **1 pound white mushrooms,** halved; **1 small red onion,** cut into 8 wedges; **2 tablespoons olive oil;** and **1 teaspoon fresh thyme leaves** until well coated. Top with **4 chicken-leg quarters;** sprinkle with **1 teaspoon salt** and ½ **teaspoon freshly ground black pepper.** Roast **35 TO 40 MINUTES** or until chicken is cooked through (165°F).

SALMON

WITH

Pea Puree

Ask your fishmonger for center-cut salmon fillets, which are of uniform thickness. That way they'll cook more evenly.

PREP	SERVES
20 *min*	**4**

In 2-quart saucepan, heat **1 teaspoon olive oil** over medium heat. Add **1 cup sliced leeks;** cook, stirring, **2 MINUTES** or until tender. Add **1½ cups frozen peas,** thawed; **½ cup dry white wine;** and ¼ *cup water;* heat to boiling, about **2 MINUTES**. Reduce heat to medium; simmer **5 TO 6 MINUTES** or until reduced by half. Meanwhile, in 12-inch nonstick skillet, heat **1 teaspoon olive oil** over medium heat **1 MINUTE**. Sprinkle **4 pieces skinless salmon fillets** (6 ounces each) with ¼ **teaspoon salt;** cook, turning once, **10 MINUTES** or until just opaque in center. While fish cooks, puree pea mixture in blender with ¼ **cup half-and-half,** ¼ **teaspoon salt,** and ¼ **teaspoon freshly ground black pepper.** Serve with salmon.

KITCHEN HACK

Quick-thaw the peas by placing them in a strainer and rinsing with warm water.

SHRIMP

& Rice

For an instant taste of the bayou, after sautéing the veggies, add ½ teaspoon Cajun or Creole seasoning and cook 30 seconds.

PREP
15
min

SERVES
4

In 12-inch nonstick skillet, heat **1 tablespoon olive oil** over medium heat. Add **1 small onion,** chopped, and **1 red pepper,** chopped; cook, stirring occasionally, **5 MINUTES** or until tender. Stir in **1 clove garlic,** minced, and **1 cup long-grain white rice;** cook **1 MINUTE**. Add **1 can (10¾ ounces) cream of celery soup** and *2 cups water;* heat to boiling, **3 TO 5 MINUTES**. Reduce heat to low; cover and simmer **10 MINUTES**. Stir in **1 pound frozen shelled raw shrimp;** cover and cook, stirring once, **12 MINUTES** or until rice is just tender. Fluff with fork.

TUNA

WITH

Blood Orange Salsa

Blood oranges, noted for their bright red flesh, have an intense orange flavor with a hint of raspberry. They are available in the supermarket produce section from January through mid-April.

PREP
20
min

SERVES
4

In large bowl, combine **3 blood oranges,** peeled and diced; **1½ cups finely chopped fennel; 3 tablespoons chopped green olives; 1 tablespoon extra-virgin olive oil; ¼ teaspoon salt;** and **¼ teaspoon freshly ground black pepper.** Sprinkle **4 tuna steaks,** each ¾-inch thick (1¼ pounds total), with **¼ teaspoon salt** and **¼ teaspoon freshly ground pepper.** In 10-inch cast-iron or other heavy skillet, heat **2 tablespoons extra-virgin olive oil** over medium-high heat. Add tuna, and cook, turning once, **6 MINUTES** or until pale pink in center (medium) or desired doneness. Serve with salsa.

TOMATOES

*When it comes to quick, creative cooking,
tomatoes top the talent bar.*

TOMATO TIME

For best-quality tomatoes it pays to visit the farmers' market, because once a tomato is ripe and ready to be picked, it is extremely fragile and loses its flavor within a few days. While supermarket tomatoes are harvested prior to fully ripening so they can be shipped long distances, only a local farmer can pick them at their peak and bring them quickly to the market. Here are some varieties to look for.

BEEFSTEAK The perfect tomato for burgers and anytime you want a large, firm slice of tomato.

CHERRY Tiny super-sweet tomatoes that range from pea-sized up to small "salad" type. Varieties include "Sweet 100" and "Grape Tomato" (more oblong than a traditional cherry tomato). Good used whole in salads, for roasting and in pastas.

PLUM Thick flesh and less pulp make this variety excellent for slicing and quick-cooking sauces.

HEIRLOOM Old regional varieties that have been saved or maintained over many generations. They can be prized for their extra-large size, unusual coloring, or special connoisseur flavors. Best eaten raw with olive oil, vinegar, and a sprinkle of salt or freshly ground black pepper.

Chicken & Tomato
SAUTÉ

Try this dish with grape tomatoes, cherry, or mixed baby heirlooms.

PREP	SERVES
15	**4**
min	

Cut **1½ pounds chicken tenders** into 1-inch chunks; sprinkle with **½ teaspoon salt** and **½ teaspoon freshly ground black pepper**. In 12-inch skillet, melt **2 tablespoons butter or margarine** over medium-high heat. Add chicken; cook **2 MINUTES** or until browned. Turn chicken over; add **1 cup snugly packed pitted prunes, 1 pint grape tomatoes, 1 tablespoon red wine vinegar,** and *¼ cup water*. Cook, stirring occasionally, **3 TO 4 MINUTES** or just until chicken is no longer pink and some tomatoes burst.

Hearty
PANZANELLA

Thin strips of salami add zip to this classic Italian tomato and bread salad.

PREP	SERVES
15	**6**
min	

Preheat oven to 375°F. Cut ends from **1 loaf baguette** (10 ounces); discard. Cut remaining bread into ½-inch cubes; place on cookie sheet and bake **8 MINUTES** or until toasted. Cool completely. In large bowl, toss **4 medium tomatoes,** cut into ½-inch chunks; **2 cups (½-inch chunks) seedless (English) cucumber;** and **⅔ cup Balsamic Vinaigrette** (p. 95). Add bread cubes; **1 package (3 ounces) sliced salami,** cut into thin strips; and **1½ cups loosely packed fresh basil leaves,** torn; toss to coat.

Fresh Tomato
PASTA

Meaty plum tomatoes are perfect for this no-cook pasta sauce.

PREP	SERVES
20	**4**
min	

Cook **1 pound bowtie pasta** in *boiling salted water* as package label directs, **9 TO 11 MINUTES**. Drain well; return to pot. Meanwhile, in large bowl, toss **2 pounds ripe tomatoes,** chopped; **3 green onions,** sliced; **¼ cup Kalamata olives,** pitted and chopped; **1 tablespoon olive brine; ¾ teaspoon salt;** and **¼ teaspoon freshly ground black pepper**. Toss with pasta; stir in **1 log (4 ounces) goat cheese,** crumbled.

147

Chicken-Watermelon
TACOS

Watermelon stands in for typical tomatoes in these sensational tacos. Look for mild and creamy Cotija cheese in Hispanic markets. Otherwise, sub in feta cheese.

PREP
15
min

SERVES
4

Toss **2 cups diced seedless watermelon; 1 jalapeño chile,** minced; **½ small red onion,** minced; **¼ cup fresh lime juice; ¼ cup fresh cilantro leaves and stems,** chopped; and **¼ teaspoon salt.** Serve on **8 corn tortillas,** warmed, with **1 pound grilled chicken,** sliced, and **2 ounces Cotija cheese,** crumbled.

KITCHEN HACK

Purchase grilled chicken cutlets from the deli department at the supermarket.

Crunchy
PRETZEL
CHICKEN

A DIY mustard dressing does double duty as both a chicken coating and a zesty dipping sauce.

PREP	SERVES
15	**4**
min	

Preheat oven to 400°F. Place wire rack in large jelly-roll pan. In medium bowl, stir together **½ cup Dijon mustard with seeds, 3 tablespoons balsamic vinegar, 3 tablespoons olive oil,** and **⅛ teaspoon freshly ground black pepper;** set aside ½ cup mixture. Spread remaining all over **4 medium skinless, boneless chicken-breast halves** (1½ pounds total). Press **2 cups pretzels,** coarsely crushed, on chicken to coat; place on rack. Bake **25 MINUTES** or until chicken is cooked through (165°F). Serve with mustard sauce.

CHICKEN

WITH

Radish Relish

A touch of prepared horseradish gives the peppery radish relish extra kick.

PREP
15
min

SERVES
4

Prepare outdoor grill for direct grilling over medium-high heat. Sprinkle **1 pound skinless, boneless chicken thighs** with **¼ teaspoon salt** and **¼ teaspoon freshly ground black pepper.** Place chicken on grill; cover and cook, turning once, **10 MINUTES** or until chicken is cooked through (165°F). Meanwhile, in food processor, with knife blade attached, pulse **6 radishes,** trimmed; **¼ cup packed fresh flat-leaf parsley leaves; 3 tablespoons sweet relish; 2 teaspoons prepared horseradish; and ⅛ teaspoon freshly ground black pepper** until finely chopped. Spoon relish over chicken.

KITCHEN HACK

Save time by cooking the chicken in a grill pan on the stove top.

Mom's
MAC 'N' CHEESE

This bubbly, gooey, and oh-so-cheesy dish is sure to satisfy the most avid comfort food fan.

PREP
15
min

SERVES
4

8 ounces ziti pasta
2 tablespoons butter or margarine
1 small onion, finely chopped
1 tablespoon all-purpose flour
¾ teaspoon dry mustard
1 teaspoon salt
⅛ teaspoon freshly ground black pepper
1½ cups milk
1 package (8 ounces) shredded sharp
   Cheddar cheese

1. Preheat oven to 350°F. Grease 9-inch square baking dish or casserole.

2. In 3-quart saucepan, cook pasta in *boiling salted water* as package label directs, **9 TO 11 MINUTES**. Drain well.

3. In same saucepan, melt butter over medium heat. Add onion and cook **5 MINUTES** or until tender. Add flour, mustard, salt, and pepper; stir until blended. Gradually stir in milk; cook, stirring, **8 TO 10 MINUTES** or until thickened. Remove from heat; stir in cheese until melted.

4. Spoon pasta into prepared baking dish. Pour cheese sauce over pasta. Bake **20 MINUTES** or until bubbly.

Take Mom's Mac 'n' Cheese (before baking), and make more magic with these 10-minute stir-ins and toppers. Try any recipe using penne or medium shells. All recipes make 4 servings.

CHESAPEAKE BAY MAC 'N' CHEESE

Stir **¾ cup lump crabmeat,** picked over; **¼ cup snipped fresh chives;** and **1 teaspoon Old Bay seasoning** into mac 'n' cheese. Top with **crushed oyster crackers.**

SAUSAGE PIE MAC 'N' CHEESE

Sauté **1 cup crumbled sausage** and **2 cups sliced mushrooms** in 12-inch skillet until cooked; toss with mac 'n' cheese and **1 medium diced tomato.**

LEAN GREEN MAC 'N' CHEESE

Stir **1 cup baby spinach, 1 cup thawed frozen peas,** and **1 cup steamed small broccoli florets** into mac 'n' cheese.

BACON—RED PEPPER MAC 'N' CHEESE

Stir **5 slices cooked crumbled bacon, ½ cup sliced green onion,** and **¼ cup chopped roasted red pepper** into mac 'n' cheese.

MMMMM, MAC 'N' CHEESE

Follow these simple rules for perfect mac 'n' cheese every time.

USE THE RIGHT PASTA Like ziti, macaroni elbows are designed to hold thick creamy sauces. Cheese sauce is too heavy for delicate shapes like cappellini, causing them to become limp and unmanageable.

COOK THE PASTA UNTIL AL DENTE Translation: Firm to the bite. Overcooked pasta will turn to mush as the casserole bakes, so stick to the package directions, using the shorter cooking time if there's a range.

STICK TO BASIC CHEESE Sharp Cheddar delivers the flavor you crave, so leave the fancy stuff for the cheese plate. If you want your mac extra creamy substitute half the Cheddar for Monterey Jack cheese.

GIVE IT A REST Let the dish stand 15 minutes for easier serving.

ZUCCHINI

When it comes to speedy meals, make this quickest-cooking member of the squash family your go-to veggie.

SQUASH ANYONE?

Summer squash—aka zucchini, yellow squash, and crookneck squash—has a flavor range from nutty to buttery to cucumber-like. While it's easy to be tempted to buy zucchini by the bucket-full when in peak season, keep in mind yellow summer squash doesn't store well. If not using zukes right away, wrap in paper towels, then plastic wrap, and chill in the refrigerator crisper drawer no more than a few days.

Creamy
CHICKEN SAUTÉ

This dish is perfect to try with a colorful mix of green and yellow zucchini.

PREP
15
min

SERVES
4

In 12-inch skillet, heat **1 tablespoon olive oil** over medium-high heat. Add **1 pound skinless, boneless chicken breasts,** cut into 1-inch chunks, and sprinkle with **¼ teaspoon salt** and **¼ teaspoon freshly ground black pepper.** Cook, stirring occasionally, **3 TO 4 MINUTES** or just until golden on all sides. Stir in **2 yellow squash,** chopped; cook **3 MINUTES** or just until tender. Stir in **¼ cup heavy or whipping cream** and **2 tablespoons white wine vinegar.** Reduce heat to low and cook **3 MINUTES** or until sauce thickens.

Veggie
MINI MEATLOAVES

The addition of shredded zucchini makes these loaves extra moist and tender.

PREP
20
min

SERVES
4

Preheat oven to 425°F. Spray jelly-roll pan with nonstick cooking spray. Coarsely shred **¾ pound zucchini.** Squeeze until very dry. In large bowl, with hands, mix zucchini, **1 pound 85% lean ground beef, ⅓ cup seasoned dried bread crumbs, 1 large egg, 2 tablespoons ketchup, ¼ teaspoon salt,** and **¼ teaspoon freshly ground black pepper** just until well blended but not overmixed. Shape into 4 loaves (each 5″ by 3″) on pan; spread tops with **3 tablespoons ketchup.** Bake **25 MINUTES** or until instant-read thermometer inserted in centers reaches 160°F.

TUNA *Tomato* LINGUINE

Zucchini ribbons require no cooking because they're tossed with hot pasta (and the zesty tuna-caper sauce is no-cook too).

PREP
15
min

SERVES
6

Cook **1 pound linguine** in *boiling salted water* as package label directs, **9 TO 11 MINUTES**. Meanwhile, with vegetable peeler, shave **1 pound zucchini** to form wide ribbons. Stop peeling when you reach seeds; discard. Drain pasta. Toss with zucchini; **2 cans (5 ounces each) tuna in olive oil,** undrained; **1 pint cherry tomatoes,** cut in half; **2 tablespoons capers,** rinsed and chopped; **¼ teaspoon salt;** and **¼ teaspoon freshly ground black pepper.**

KITCHEN HACK

Use a swivel-head Y-shaped vegetable peeler to shave the zucchini into ribbons.

157

GREEK PIZZA
Pockets

Prepared pizza dough makes these calzone-style sandwiches a breeze to assemble. Try whole-wheat dough for a subtle nutty flavor.

PREP
20
min

SERVES
4

Preheat oven to 425°F. In bowl, stir **1 package (10 ounces) frozen chopped spinach,** thawed and squeezed dry; **1 container (15 ounces) ricotta cheese;** 2/3 cup crumbled tomato-basil feta cheese; and **3 tablespoons chopped fresh dill.** Divide **1 pound refrigerated pizza dough** into 4 pieces; on floured board, press each into 8″ by 7″ oval. Spoon one-fourth of filling on center of each oval; brush edges with water. Fold each over lengthwise to enclose filling; press to seal. Place on cookie sheet; cut slit in each. Bake until golden brown, **25 MINUTES**.

EGGPLANT
Sandwiches

Talk about sammie bliss! Sliced eggplant is grilled until sweet and smoky, then stacked with tomato and fresh mozzarella on chewy Italian ciabbata.

PREP
20 *min*

SERVES
4

Prepare outdoor grill for direct grilling over medium-high heat. In large bowl, toss **1 medium eggplant,** cut into ½-inch slices, with **2 tablespoons balsamic vinegar; 2 tablespoons olive oil; ½ teaspoon salt;** and **¼ teaspoon freshly ground black pepper** until well coated. Place eggplant on grill; cook, turning once, **5 TO 7 MINUTES** or until very tender. Layer eggplant; **1 medium tomato,** sliced; **4 ounces fresh mozzarella,** sliced; and **1 small bunch fresh basil,** leaves removed, on bottom of 1 (12-inch) loaf ciabatta or other Italian bread, split horizontally. Drizzle with **2 teaspoons balsamic vinegar;** replace top. Cut into 4 sandwiches.

CORN
&
BEAN
Burgers

These veggie burgers get their oomph from shredded sharp Cheddar cheese mixed right into each patty.

PREP
15 *min*

SERVES
4

In food processor, with knife blade attached, pulse **1 can (15 ounces) pink beans,** drained and rinsed well; **½ cup plain dried bread crumbs; ¼ teaspoon salt;** and **¼ teaspoon freshly ground black pepper** until ground. Add **1 cup corn kernels** and **½ cup shredded sharp Cheddar cheese;** pulse to just combine. Divide into 4 portions and shape into 4-inch patties. In 12-inch nonstick skillet, heat **1 teaspoon vegetable oil** over medium heat. Add patties; spray with nonstick cooking spray. Cook, turning once, **15 MINUTES** or until browned. Serve on **hamburger buns** with **lettuce** and **sliced tomato.**

PUNCH IT UP!
Meatballs

MEATBALL PIZZA

For the crispiest crust, bake this hearty pie on the lowest oven rack.

Heat cookie sheet in 450°F oven. On parchment, shape **1 pound pizza dough** into 14-inch oval. Place on hot cookie sheet. Top with **1 cup marinara sauce;** ½ bag meatballs; **¼ cup giardiniera; 1 package (8 ounces) Italian-blend shredded cheese;** and ⅓ **cup fresh basil leaves,** torn; bake **20 MINUTES** or until bottom is crisp. **SERVES 6.**

·············

SWEDISH MEATBALLS

Melt **3 tablespoons butter or margarine** in large skillet over medium heat. Add **1 chopped onion,** and cook **5 MINUTES** or until tender. Stir in **2 tablespoons flour** until blended. Stir in 1 bag meatballs, **1 can (14½ ounces) beef broth, 2 tablespoons heavy or whipping cream, 2 teaspoons fresh lemon juice,** and **2 teaspoons Worcestershire sauce.** Simmer **7 MINUTES** or until bubbly. **SERVES 6.**

News flash: A (16-ounce) bag of frozen meatballs isn't just for spaghetti—and these 10-minute-to-prep recipes are the delicious proof.

MEATBALL ENCHILADAS

If you like enchiladas extra spicy, use shredded pepper Jack cheese.

Preheat oven to 400°F. In large bowl, mix **1 can (8 ounces) tomato sauce, 1 tablespoon chili powder,** and 1 bag meatballs. Fill **8 corn tortillas** with meatball mixture; put seam side down in baking dish. Top with **1 can (10 ounces) enchilada sauce** and **1 package (8 ounces) Mexican-blend shredded cheese;** bake **30 MINUTES** or until bubbly. **SERVES 4.**

·············

MOROCCAN MEATBALLS

In large saucepan, heat **1 tablespoon olive oil** over medium heat. Add **1 chopped onion** and cook **5 MINUTES** or until tender. Add **1 (28-ounce) can tomato puree,** 1 bag meatballs, **1 cup beef broth, 1 tablespoon ground cumin,** and **¼ teaspoon ground cinnamon;** simmer **10 MINUTES**. **SERVES 8.**

Meatball Pizza

STONE FRUITS

Sweet, juicy, and utterly delicious peaches, nectarines, and plums share one thing in common: a hard, large pit (or "stone"). They're also fabulous in savory dishes, requiring little cooking (or none at all).

PLUM GOOD TIPS

These handy hints work for peaches and nectarines too!

HOW TO CHOOSE For peaches and nectarines, trust your nose: The fruit should smell ripe and delicious. Plums should be deeply colored, shiny, and firm (but not hard).

HOW TO PIT Cut the fruit lengthwise in half, following the cleft that runs down one side. Twist the halves in opposite directions to free the pit. If the fruit is ripe, it should pop right out.

NOT RIPE YET? Patience required. Leave the fruit at room temperature (not in the fridge) for a few days.

Peachy GRILLED CHICKEN

What's the best thing about grilled peaches (aside from fabulous flavor)? You don't have to peel them.

PREP | **SERVES**
20 *min* | **4**

Preheat grill for medium-high heat. In large bowl, mix **½ cup mint leaves,** finely chopped; **2 cloves garlic,** finely chopped; **2 teaspoons grated lemon peel; ¼ teaspoon salt;** and **¼ teaspoon black pepper.** Add **1 pound peaches,** halved; toss to coat. Transfer peaches to plate. Toss **1¼ pounds boneless, skinless chicken thighs** with mint mixture. Place chicken on grill. Cook, turning once, **8 TO 10 MINUTES** or until instant-read thermometer inserted horizontally into thickest part of chicken reaches 165°F. Place peaches on grill; cook, turning once, **5 MINUTES** or until grill marks appear. Serve chicken with peaches.

SALMON with Plum Salsa

While the salmon zaps in the microwave, whip up the salsa and you're good to go.

PREP | **SERVES**
20 *min* | **4**

In 9-inch glass pie plate, arrange **4 pieces skinless salmon fillet** (6 ounces each), rounded sides down, with thinner ends toward center; sprinkle with **¼ teaspoon salt** and **⅛ teaspoon freshly ground black pepper.** Cover with vented plastic wrap and microwave on High **5 MINUTES** or until just opaque in center. Meanwhile, in medium bowl, mix **6 medium plums,** diced; **1 cup chopped English (seedless) cucumber; 2 tablespoons chopped fresh cilantro; 2 tablespoons fresh lime juice;** and **¼ teaspoon salt.** Serve salsa with salmon.

TURKEY & NECTARINE Toss

Smoked turkey and juicy sweet nectarines make a terrific flavor combo in this no-cook meal.

PREP | **SERVES**
20 *min* | **4**

In large bowl, toss **2 pounds nectarines,** thinly sliced, with **12 ounces smoked turkey breast,** diced; **3 cups herb salad greens; 4 radishes,** thinly sliced; **2 tablespoons fresh lime juice; ¼ teaspoon salt;** and **⅛ teaspoon freshly ground black pepper** until well combined.

KITCHEN HACK

Buy a single piece of smoked turkey breast from the deli counter; it will be easier to dice than the packaged sliced stuff.

EASY SPAGHETTI
Carbonara

Call this pasta classic with cheese, bacon, and eggs comfort food Italian-style. We add color and freshness with a handful of green peas.

PREP	SERVES
15 *min*	**6**

In saucepot, cook **1 pound spaghetti** in *boiling salted water* 2 MINUTES less than package label directs, **7 TO 9 MINUTES**. Add **2 cups frozen peas;** cook **2 MINUTES**. Reserve *½ cup cooking water;* drain pasta and peas. Meanwhile, in 12-inch skillet, cook **6 slices bacon,** chopped, over medium heat **8 MINUTES** or until browned; reserve fat. In large bowl, with wire whisk, beat **4 large eggs, ½ cup freshly grated Pecorino Romano cheese,** 2 tablespoons reserved bacon fat, reserved cooking water, **½ teaspoon salt,** and **½ teaspoon freshly ground black pepper.** Toss in pasta mixture and bacon.

Red Wine
SPAGHETTI

Cooking the pasta in a skillet means you don't have to wait for a large pot of water to come to a boil.

PREP	SERVES
5 *min*	**2**

In 12-inch skillet, stir together **2 cups red wine,** *2 cups water,* and **½ teaspoon salt.** Add **8 ounces thin spaghetti.** Heat to boiling, stirring, over high heat, **8 TO 10 MINUTES**. Boil, stirring often, **9 TO 11 MINUTES** or until pasta is tender. Remove from heat. Stir in **1 tablespoon capers,** drained and chopped; **1 tablespoon butter or margarine;** and **⅛ teaspoon freshly ground black pepper.** Top with **2 tablespoons freshly grated Pecorino Romano cheese.**

PENNE WITH
Pistachio Pesto

Flat-leaf parsley subs in for basil for a pesto sauce you can make any time of year.

PREP	SERVES
20 *min*	**4**

Cook **1 pound penne** in *boiling salted water* as package label directs, **9 TO 11 MINUTES**. Meanwhile, in food processor, with knife blade attached, pulse **2 cups fresh flat-leaf parsley leaves; 1 cup roasted, salted pistachios,** shelled; **¼ cup freshly grated Parmesan cheese; 1 clove garlic; ¼ teaspoon salt;** and **⅛ teaspoon freshly ground black pepper** until combined. With processor running, add **⅔ cup extra-virgin olive oil** until smooth. Drain pasta well. In large bowl, toss pasta with pesto.

Easy Spaghetti Carbonara

PUNCH IT UP!
Shredded Carrots

SLOPPY TOMS

This big-batch recipe makes enough for 8 hot sammies with only 10 minutes of prep. Or serve half the recipe, and freeze the remaining filling for another quickie meal.

In 12-inch skillet, cook **1 pound ground dark-meat turkey** over medium-high heat **4 TO 5 MINUTES** or until browned, breaking it up with side of spoon. Stir in shredded carrots, **2 teaspoons chili powder, ¼ teaspoon salt,** and **⅛ teaspoon freshly ground black pepper;** cook, stirring occasionally, **2 MINUTES.** Add **1 can (28 ounces) stewed tomatoes;** crush with back of spoon. Heat to boiling, **3 TO 5 MINUTES.** Cook, stirring occasionally, **12 TO 15 MINUTES** or until thickened. Divide among **8 hamburger buns,** toasted. **SERVES 8.**

Take a package of shredded carrots (8 or 10 ounces will do the trick), grab your favorite skillet, and you've got two fabulous suppers.

PEPPER BEEF SIZZLE

This simple, four-serving, fifteen-minute prep stir-fry is also delicious with pork tenderloin.

In large bowl, combine **1 beef flank steak** (1 pound), very thinly sliced, and **2 tablespoons oyster sauce.** In 12-inch skillet, heat **2 teaspoons vegetable oil** over high heat until hot. Add beef in single layer. Cook **1 MINUTE** or until browned on bottom; transfer to plate. In same skillet, heat **1 teaspoon vegetable oil** over medium-high heat. Add **1 bunch green onions,** cut into 1-inch pieces. Cook, stirring, **2 MINUTES** or until lightly browned. Add shredded carrots and *2 tablespoons water;* cook, stirring, **2 MINUTES** or until crisp-tender. Return beef to skillet, along with **½ teaspoon coarsely ground black pepper** and **2 tablespoons oyster sauce.** Cook, stirring, **1 MINUTE.** **SERVES 4.**

KITCHEN HACK

Skip the knife work and buy beef pre-sliced for stir-fry.

SIDE

Attractions

Our treasure trove of express-lane
sides will make the meal.

Braised
RED CABBAGE

Apple cider replaces the typical sugar in this easy spin on sweet and sour cabbage.

PREP
10
min

SERVES
4

In 12-inch skillet, heat **1 tablespoon olive oil** over medium-high heat. Add **1 small head red cabbage,** thinly sliced, and **½ teaspoon salt.** Cook, stirring, **2 MINUTES.** Add **1 cup apple cider** and **2 tablespoons cider vinegar.** Heat to boiling, **3 TO 5 MINUTES.** Reduce heat to medium-low. Cover and simmer **20 MINUTES** or until tender. Stir in **1 tablespoon capers,** chopped.

KITCHEN HACK

Skip the knife work and use 2 (8-ounce) packages of shredded red cabbage.

Melted
SAVOY CABBAGE
WITH
HERBS

Savoy cabbage, with deeply wrinkled, extra-tender leaves, is prized for its mildly earthy, sweet taste.

PREP
15
min

SERVES
4

In 5-quart saucepot, heat **2 tablespoons butter or margarine** and **1 tablespoon olive oil** over medium heat. Add **1 small onion,** thinly sliced; cook, stirring, **3 MINUTES.** Stir in **1 head savoy cabbage,** thinly sliced; *½ cup water;* and **¼ teaspoon salt.** Reduce heat to medium-low. Cover and cook, stirring occasionally, **15 TO 20 MINUTES** or until cabbage is very tender. Remove from heat. Stir in **3 green onions,** thinly sliced; **1 tablespoon fresh tarragon leaves,** finely chopped; and **⅛ teaspoon freshly ground black pepper.**

Melted Savoy Cabbage with Herbs

Crispy
PARMESAN
BROCCOLI

Roasting brings out the natural sweetness in broccoli; panko bread crumbs give the topping extra crunch.

PREP
10
min

SERVES
4

Preheat oven to 450°F. In large jelly-roll pan, toss together **1 pound broccoli florets** with **1 tablespoon olive oil, ¼ teaspoon salt,** and **¼ teaspoon freshly ground black pepper** until well coated. Spread in single layer. Roast **15 MINUTES**. Meanwhile, in small bowl, combine **¼ cup freshly grated Parmesan cheese, ¼ cup panko bread crumbs, 2 teaspoons olive oil,** and **1 teaspoon finely grated lemon peel.** Sprinkle panko mixture over broccoli; roast **3 TO 5 MINUTES** or until broccoli is tender and crumbs are golden brown.

KITCHEN
HACK

Buy fresh broccoli florets sold in bulk from the produce section of the supermarket.

Smashing
MASHED POTATOES

Yellow-fleshed Yukon gold potatoes have a rich, almost buttery taste. If you like a slightly tangy edge to your mash, swap buttermilk for the milk.

PREP
25
min

SERVES
4-6

2 pounds Yukon Gold potatoes, peeled and cut into 1-inch chunks
½ cup warm milk
2 tablespoons butter or margarine
½ teaspoon salt

1. In 4-quart saucepan, combine potatoes and enough *cold water* to cover. Heat to boiling over high heat, **10 TO 15 MINUTES**. Reduce heat to maintain simmer. Partially cover; simmer **15 MINUTES** or until very tender.

2. Drain well and return to saucepan. Add milk, butter, and salt. Mash until smooth.

Ready to do the mash? Make a batch of Smashing Mashed Potatoes, then add a yummy 5-minute stir-in. All recipes make 4 to 6 servings.

CHEESY CHIVE MASHED POTATOES

If you're in a super time crunch, use 4 cups cooked instant mashed potatoes.

Fold **1 cup shredded extra-sharp Cheddar cheese** and **2 tablespoons snipped fresh chives** into mashed potatoes until well mixed.

ZINGY BACON MASHED POTATOES

Fold **3 slices crumbled cooked bacon, 1½ tablespoons prepared horseradish,** and **1½ tablespoons chopped fresh flat-leaf parsley** into mashed potatoes until well mixed.

SPICY 'N' SMOKY MASHED POTATOES

Fold **1 cup thawed frozen corn, ⅓ cup sour cream,** and **1 tablespoon chopped chipotles in adobo** into mashed potatoes until well mixed.

GARLICKY HERB MASHED POTATOES

Fold **2 tablespoons chopped fresh basil leaves; ½ cup freshly grated Parmesan cheese;** and **1 clove garlic,** finely chopped, into mashed potatoes until well mixed.

SPUD SAVVY

Use these smarts and you'll whip up fabulous mashed potatoes every time.

PICK THE RIGHT POTATO All-purpose, Yukon Gold, and starchy russet potatoes are preferable to waxy potatoes (like red-skinned spuds), as they are less dense and break down more during cooking. The result? Your mash will have a smoother texture.

DO A DONENESS TEST Overcooked spuds will be soupy; undercooked will have pockets of crunch. A perfectly cooked piece of potato should give no resistance when cut with a knife, while still holding its shape.

MASH WITH CARE Overmixing mashed potatoes can result in a stiff, chewy texture. Keep them fluffy by using a potato ricer for smooth spuds or use a hand-held masher for a chunkier mash (never the food processor).

POTATO GRATIN

Psst! Cream of celery soup creates a velvety rich gratin.

PREP
15
min

SERVES
4

Preheat oven to 400°F. In 4-quart saucepan, whisk together **1 can (10¾ ounces) cream of celery soup** and **¾ cup milk;** heat to boiling over medium-high heat, stirring occasionally, about **5 MINUTES**. Stir in **1 tablespoon Dijon mustard; ½ cup shredded sharp Cheddar cheese;** and **1½ pounds baking potatoes,** peeled and thinly sliced. Transfer to shallow 6-cup baking dish; sprinkle with **½ cup shredded sharp Cheddar cheese.** Bake **45 MINUTES** or until potatoes are fork-tender.

KITCHEN HACK

Slice the spuds in a food processor fitted with a slicing blade.

Stuffed
PARMESAN POTATOES

Bye-bye boring potatoes! These stuffed spuds are all dressed up for company.

PREP
20
min

SERVES
6

KITCHEN HACK

To test potatoes for doneness, a fork should easily insert in the center of each spud.

Preheat oven to 425°F. Pierce **3 unpeeled medium russet potatoes,** scrubbed, with fork. Place in 2-quart baking dish; cover with vented plastic wrap. Microwave on High **17 MINUTES** or until tender. Cut each potato crosswise in half; scoop flesh into bowl. Cut slices off bottoms of potato shells. Mash flesh with **½ cup heavy or whipping cream; ¼ cup freshly grated Parmesan cheese; 5 fresh basil leaves,** chopped; **⅛ teaspoon dried thyme; ½ teaspoon salt;** and **⅛ teaspoon freshly ground black pepper.** Spoon into potato shells; place in baking dish. Top with **¼ cup freshly grated Parmesan cheese.** Bake **15 MINUTES** or until lightly browned.

Spicy
SWEET POTATOES

These roasted spuds are glazed with maple syrup and smoky chipotle chile. Serve with grilled pork chops or steak.

PREP
15
min

SERVES
4

Preheat oven to 425°F. Line large jelly-roll pan with foil. In large bowl, toss together **2 pounds unpeeled scrubbed sweet potatoes,** each cut into 8 wedges, with **¼ cup maple syrup, 1 tablespoon vegetable oil, ½ teaspoon ground cumin,** and **½ teaspoon salt** until well coated. Arrange in single layer on prepared pan. Roast **25 TO 30 MINUTES** or until potatoes are fork-tender. Meanwhile, in blender, puree **¼ cup maple syrup, 1 chipotle chile in adobo,** and **pinch salt;** drizzle over potatoes.

Spaghetti Squash
with Olives &
Pecorino

SPAGHETTI SQUASH

WITH

Olives & Pecorino

Zap it, and this mild-tasting squash magically transforms into spaghetti-like strands.

PREP
15
min

SERVES
4

With small knife, pierce **1 small spaghetti squash** (2½ pounds) all over. On microwave-safe plate, microwave squash on High **14 MINUTES** or until tender. Cut squash in half lengthwise and let cool; discard seeds. With two forks, scrape out pulp from squash in long strands; place in medium bowl. Stir in **¼ cup pitted Kalamata olives,** chopped; **3 tablespoons freshly grated Pecorino Romano cheese; 2 tablespoons chopped fresh parsley; 1 tablespoon olive oil;** and **2 teaspoons red wine vinegar.**

Savory GLAZED SQUASH

Acorn squash gets the royal treatment roasted with fresh sage, drizzled with orange juice and honey, then topped off with crunchy bacon.

PREP
20
min

SERVES
4

Preheat oven to 450°F. In large bowl, toss together **2 small acorn squash,** seeded and cut into ¾-inch-thick half-rings, with **4 large fresh sage leaves,** chopped; **2 teaspoons vegetable oil; ¼ teaspoon salt;** and **¼ teaspoon freshly ground black pepper** until well coated. Arrange in single layer on 18- by 12-inch jelly-roll pan. Roast **25 MINUTES.** Meanwhile, in small bowl, whisk together **2 tablespoons orange juice, 1 teaspoon honey,** and **⅛ teaspoon salt.** Drizzle over squash. Top with **2 slices cooked bacon,** crumbled.

KITCHEN HACK

To prep the squash, slice ½ inch off each end and halve lengthwise through the stem. With a spoon, scoop out the seeds and membrane, then cut each half crosswise into slices for a fluted edge.

CORN

*These golden kernels add sweetness and crunch
to your favorite summmer sides.*

LEND US YOUR EARS!

When it comes to cooking or (surprise!) not cooking, just-picked summer corn has its own set of rules.

DON'T STRIP BACK THE HUSKS to pick the freshest ears (you'll just dry out the kernels). Instead, feel from the top of the ear to be sure that the kernels are filled out and go all the way to the end.

ENJOY ASAP Otherwise chill the extras in their husks for up to 2 days. The husks will keep the moisture in the kernels, and chilling will slow down the sugar-to-starch conversion, keeping the sweet taste intact.

COOK JUST UNTIL WARM ENOUGH TO MELT BUTTER The longer you cook corn, the more you toughen it, because cooking converts the corn's sugar to starch. Boiled corn on the cob can take as little as I minute, so check early and often for doneness.

Tangy CORN TOSS

Just-picked corn, straight off the cob, needs no cooking to be sweet and tender.

PREP
20
min

SERVES
4

In large bowl, whisk together ¼ **cup olive oil, 1 tablespoon red wine vinegar,** and ¼ **teaspoon salt.** Add **3 cups fresh corn kernels; 2 cups frozen edamame,** thawed; ¼ **small red onion,** minced; and ⅔ **cup freshly grated Parmesan cheese;** toss to coat.

KITCHEN HACK

One medium ear of corn yields about ½ cup of kernels, so figure 6 ears for this recipe.

Zesty GRILLED CORN

Corn on the cob is slathered in a special 'cue sauce spiked with five-spice powder and grated orange peel.

PREP
15
min

SERVES
6

Prepare outdoor grill for direct grilling over medium heat. In small bowl, stir together ½ **cup barbecue sauce, 2 tablespoons snipped fresh chives,** ½ **teaspoon Chinese five-spice powder,** ½ **teaspoon finely grated orange peel,** and ¼ **teaspoon salt.** Place **6 medium ears of corn,** husks and silk removed, on grill; cook, turning occasionally, **6 TO 7 MINUTES** or until lightly charred all over. Brush corn with sauce mixture; cook, turning often, **2 MINUTES** longer.

Summer SUCCOTASH

Sweet pickle relish adds zing to this corn and lima bean classic.

PREP
15
min

SERVES
6

In 12-inch skillet, melt **2 tablespoons butter or margarine** over medium heat. Add **2 cups chopped yellow squash,** ¼ **teaspoon salt,** and ¼ **teaspoon freshly ground black pepper.** Cook, stirring, **1 MINUTE** or just until tender. Stir in **2 cups fresh corn kernels** and **2 cups frozen lima beans.** Cover and cook, stirring occasionally, **8 TO 10 MINUTES** or until tender. Uncover and stir in **3 tablespoons sweet pickle relish.**

ARTICHOKES

WITH

Creamy Lemon Sauce

Select medium-sized artichokes for this dish. Visual hint: Think tennis ball.

PREP
15
min

SERVES
4

Fill 6-quart saucepot with *1 inch water* and steamer insert. Heat to boiling over high heat; reduce heat to medium. Place **4 artichokes,** stems trimmed, stem side down in saucepot. Cover and steam **35 MINUTES** or until knife pierces easily through base. Meanwhile, in medium bowl, stir together **⅓ cup mayonnaise, ⅓ cup plain yogurt, ¼ cup snipped fresh chives, 2 tablespoons fresh lemon juice,** *2 tablespoons water,* **1 tablespoon Dijon mustard,** and **¼ teaspoon salt.** Serve artichokes with sauce.

ALL CHOKED UP

Not sure how to eat an artichoke once it's cooked? Get your fingers ready to dig in.

PLUCK the outer leaves one by one from the bottom of the cooked artichoke.

DIP the base of a leaf in the sauce; pull through your teeth scraping off the pulp. Discard leaf.

REPEAT until you've reached the fuzzy center choke; with the tip of a spoon, remove the fuzz.

CUT the remaining solid disk of artichoke at the bottom—that's the prized ultra-tender heart.

PUNCH IT UP!
Corn Muffin Mix

ROSEMARY-OLIVE CORNBREAD

Stir **½ cup chopped pitted Kalamata olives, 1 tablespoon chopped fresh rosemary, and ¼ teaspoon crushed red pepper** into muffin mix and bake as label directs.

PEPPER JACK-BACON CORNBREAD

Stir **6 slices chopped cooked bacon, ¾ cup shredded pepper Jack cheese, and ¼ cup thinly sliced green onions** into muffin mix and bake as label directs.

---

*It's a cinch to transform corn muffin mix into company-worthy cornbread. Prepare 1 box (8½ ounces) muffin mix, add a 10-minute stir-in, then bake as label directs for an 8-inch square baking pan. (The baking time will be **20 to 25 minutes**.) All recipes make 4 servings.*

LEMON-RASPBERRY CORNBREAD

Works with blueberries too!

Stir **1 cup raspberries** and **1 teaspoon finely grated lemon peel** into muffin mix; transfer to baking pan, sprinkle with **2 tablespoons sliced almonds,** and bake as label directs.

PECAN-APRICOT CORNBREAD

Stir **¼ cup chopped pecans, ¼ cup chopped dried apricots,** and **2 tablespoons brown sugar** into muffin mix and bake as label directs.

Tomato-Herb
FOCACCIA

Refrigerated pizza dough is slathered with rosemary- and garlic-scented olive oil, topped with sliced tomatoes, then baked until golden and crisp. Serve warm with soup or a big green salad.

PREP	SERVES
15 *min*	**6**

Preheat oven to 450°F. Arrange **3 plum tomatoes,** very thinly sliced, in single layer on paper towel. Sprinkle with **⅛ teaspoon salt.** In small bowl, combine **2 tablespoons olive oil; 2 cloves garlic,** crushed with press; **2 teaspoons chopped fresh rosemary;** and **⅛ teaspoon salt.** Lightly oil 9- by 13-inch baking pan. Press **1 pound refrigerated pizza dough** into prepared pan. Spread herb oil on top. Blot tomatoes; place on top of dough. Bake **30 TO 40 MINUTES** or until crust is golden brown.

KITCHEN HACK

Before spreading the dough with herb oil, dimple the entire top of the focaccia with your fingers. The oil will seep into every nook and cranny, so the bread will have an extra crisp exterior when baked.

ASPARAGUS

WITH

Matzo Gremolata

This crunchy matzo topping with parsley, orange peel, and garlic is also terrific with roasted broccoli.

PREP
15
min

SERVES
4

Preheat oven to 450°F. Toss together **1 bunch thin asparagus,** trimmed, with **1 tablespoon olive oil, 1/4 teaspoon salt,** and **1/4 teaspoon freshly ground black pepper** in 18- by 12-inch jelly-roll pan until well coated. Spread in single layer. In small bowl, combine **1/2 cup finely crushed matzos** (or other plain crackers) with **1 tablespoon olive oil, 1/8 teaspoon salt,** and **1/8 teaspoon freshly ground black pepper.** Sprinkle over asparagus. Roast **10 MINUTES** or until browned. Meanwhile, in small bowl, mix **1/4 cup fresh flat-leaf parsley,** finely chopped; **1 small clove garlic,** finely chopped; and **1/2 teaspoon slivered or finely grated orange peel.** Sprinkle over asparagus.

Buttery MINTED PEAS

Consider this springtime classic as the perfect accompaniment to Easter ham or lamb.

PREP
25
min

SERVES
4

In 10-inch skillet, melt **1 tablespoon butter or margarine** over medium-low heat. Add **1 small sweet onion,** minced, and ¼ **teaspoon salt;** cook, stirring, **8 MINUTES** or until golden. Meanwhile, in 4-quart saucepan, heat *¼ cup water* to boiling. Add **3 cups shelled fresh peas (from 2½ pounds pods).** Reduce heat to medium and simmer, stirring, **10 MINUTES** or until peas are tender and water has evaporated. Add onion mixture, **1 tablespoon butter or margarine,** ½ **teaspoon salt,** and ¼ **teaspoon freshly ground black pepper.** Cook, stirring, **2 MINUTES** or until peas are glazed. Stir in **2 tablespoons thinly sliced fresh mint leaves** and **1 tablespoon chopped fresh dill.**

KITCHEN HACK

To quickly shell fresh peas, split open a pod and run your thumb down its length. The peas will pop right out.

Indian-Spiced PEAS

Quick-serve frozen peas are sautéed in a fragrant combo of cumin and mustard seeds.

PREP
5
min

SERVES
4

In 12-inch skillet, heat **1 tablespoon vegetable oil** over medium-high heat. Add **1 small onion,** thinly sliced; cook, stirring, **3 MINUTES** or until browned. Stir in ½ **teaspoon cumin seeds** and ½ **teaspoon mustard seeds;** cook **30 SECONDS.** Add **1 package (10 ounces) frozen peas,** *1 tablespoon water,* ¼ **teaspoon salt,** and **pinch ground red pepper (cayenne).** Cook, stirring, **6 MINUTES** or until hot.

Indian-Spiced Peas

Braised
MUSHROOMS

Go fancy and pair this quickie side with broiled beef tenderloin steaks (aka filet mignon).

PREP
10
min

SERVES
4

In 10-inch skillet, melt **2 tablespoons butter or margarine** over medium heat. Add **1 shallot,** chopped, and **3 large fresh sage leaves;** cook **2 MINUTES.** Add **1 cup dry red wine,** **¼ teaspoon salt,** and **¼ teaspoon freshly ground black pepper.** Increase heat to high and boil **1 MINUTE.** Stir in **1 pound cremini mushrooms,** halved. Reduce heat to medium. Cover; cook **5 MINUTES.** Uncover; cook, stirring, **12 MINUTES** or until tender.

CRAZY FOR CREMINI

Except for their brown hue, cremini (aka baby portobello) mushrooms look almost identical their white cultivated cousins. But 'shroom for 'shroom they have twice the amount of flavor. So if you're serious about intense mushroom taste, substitute at least half of the amount of white mushrooms with creminis in recipes.

RED QUINOA
Pilaf

Feel free to substitute white or black quinoa if it's more readily available; all varieties have a similar taste.

PREP	SERVES
15	**4**
min	

In 2-quart saucepan, cook **1 cup rinsed red quinoa,** stirring, over medium-high heat **3 MINUTES** or until fragrant and popping. Stir in *1½ cups water.* Heat to boiling over high heat. Reduce heat to low; cover and simmer **15 MINUTES** or until water is absorbed. Transfer to large bowl and toss with **2 green onions,** thinly sliced; **¼ teaspoon salt;** and **¼ teaspoon freshly ground black pepper.** Cool slightly. Toss with **½ cup roasted, salted cashews,** coarsely chopped; **¼ cup golden raisins;** and **1 teaspoon extra-virgin olive oil.**

KITCHEN HACK

Toasting quinoa in a dry skillet heightens its nutty flavor.

Roasted APRICOTS & PISTACHIOS

Firm and sweet-tart, fresh apricots are perfect for roasting. To select ripe fruit, look for a deep, uniform golden color—especially around the stem end.

PREP	SERVES
15 *min*	**4**

Preheat oven to 350°F. Line 15½- by 10½-inch jelly-roll pan with foil. Place **8 fresh apricots,** halved and pitted, cut sides up, on prepared pan; sprinkle with **1 tablespoon sugar.** Roast **20 MINUTES** or until tender and browned. Divide **2 ounces goat cheese,** crumbled, among hot apricots; sprinkle with **½ cup salted pistachios,** toasted and chopped, and **1 tablespoon fresh mint leaves,** chopped.

Roasted BEETS IN ORANGE VINAIGRETTE

Try this dish with golden beets if available. While not as common as their magenta counterparts, they're even sweeter (and less messy to peel because their flesh won't stain).

PREP	SERVES
20 *min*	**4**

Preheat oven to 400°F. Trim and scrub **6 medium beets.** On large sheet foil, toss together beets with **1 teaspoon olive oil** and **1 whole clove garlic.** Wrap tightly; roast in pan **1 HOUR** or until knife easily pierces beets. Let cool; peel and cut into wedges. Place on platter; drizzle with any juices left in foil. Peel roasted garlic and place in small bowl. Mash with fork, then stir in **2 tablespoons olive oil, ½ teaspoon finely grated orange peel, ¼ cup fresh orange juice, ¼ teaspoon salt,** and **¼ teaspoon freshly ground black pepper.** Drizzle over beets. Sprinkle with **¼ cup fresh cilantro leaves.**

PUNCH IT UP!
Rice Pilaf Mix

—

*Add pizzazz to ho-hum rice—and cook it perfectly too. Prepare 1 (6- to 7-ounce) box of rice pilaf mix as the package directs (the cooking time will be **25 minutes**), then fold in these 10-minute flavor boosters. All recipes make 4 servings.*

—

PECAN & GOLDEN RAISIN RICE PILAF

Fluff the cooked rice lightly with a fork before adding the stir-ins.

Stir **½ cup toasted and chopped pecans, ½ cup golden raisins,** and **⅛ teaspoon ground nutmeg** into cooked rice pilaf mix until well blended.

PEA & HERB RICE PILAF

Fold **⅔ cup thawed frozen peas, ½ cup finely chopped fresh mint,** and **½ cup finely chopped fresh flat-leaf parsley** into cooked rice pilaf mix until well blended.

SPICED RED PEPPER PILAF

Fold **⅓ cup finely chopped roasted red pepper, 2 sliced green onions,** and **⅛ teaspoon ground cumin** into cooked rice pilaf mix until well blended.

SAVORY RED ONION PILAF

Fold **3 tablespoons finely chopped red onion** and **2 tablespoons coarsely chopped capers** into cooked rice pilaf mix until well blended.

Roasted CARROTS & PARSNIPS

Sweetened with a touch of honey, this is a great starter dish if your family hasn't tried parsnips before.

PREP
20
min

SERVES
4

Preheat oven to 450°F. Line large jelly-roll pan with foil. In large bowl, toss together **1 pound carrots,** peeled and sliced on an angle, with **1 pound parsnips,** peeled and sliced on an angle; **1 shallot,** finely chopped; **1 tablespoon honey; 1 tablespoon butter or margarine,** melted; **1 teaspoon olive oil; ¼ teaspoon salt;** and **⅛ teaspoon ground red pepper (cayenne)** until well coated. Arrange in single layer on prepared pan. Roast **15 MINUTES** or until tender.

Parmesan
BRUSSELS SPROUTS

To prep fresh Brussels sprouts, cut off the base of the sprout, then remove any damaged or tough outer leaves.

PREP
15
min

SERVES
4

Preheat oven to 450°F. In large jelly-roll pan, toss together **1¼ pounds Brussels sprouts,** thinly sliced; **2 tablespoons olive oil; 1 teaspoon fresh thyme leaves; 1 clove garlic,** thinly sliced; **⅛ teaspoon salt;** and **¼ teaspoon freshly ground black pepper** until well coated. Spread in single layer on prepared pan. Roast, stirring once, **20 MINUTES** or just until tender. Toss with **1 teaspoon red wine vinegar** and **¼ cup coarsely grated Parmesan cheese.**

SUGAR
Rush

These real-deal sweets
truly beat the clock.

SALTED CARAMEL
Bark

Why buy fancy chocolates when you can whip up these candies in minutes? Use bittersweet instead of semisweet chocolate if you're a dark chocolate fan.

PREP	SERVES
15 *min*	**8**

Preheat oven to 350°F. Line large jelly-roll pan with parchment paper. In large bowl, combine **3 tablespoons corn syrup, 2 tablespoons sugar,** and ¼ **teaspoon salt.** Stir in **2 cups roasted peanuts** to evenly coat. Spread in single layer on prepared pan. Bake **15 MINUTES** or until browned and caramelized. Cool completely then break into pieces. Stir into **12 ounces semisweet chocolate,** melted, until well coated. Spread evenly on waxed paper–lined pan. Refrigerate at least **1 HOUR** or until set.

KITCHEN HACK

To melt the chocolate, chop it into ½-inch pieces and transfer to a medium microwave-safe bowl. Microwave on Medium 1 to 1½ minutes; stir. If the chocolate is not melted, continue microwaving in 30-second increments, stirring occasionally, until smooth.

STRAWBERRIES

Sweet, juicy, and wildly flavorful—if a speedy dessert stars strawberries, it's bound to be sensational.

BERRY SATISFYING

Get the deets for buying the best strawberries.

PICK BRIGHT RED (NOT ORANGE OR GREEN) STRAWBERRIES, since they don't ripen once they're off the vine.

CHECK THE UNDERSIDE OF THE BASKET, making sure the berries aren't wet, which can lead to mold.

AVOID TOO MANY BERRIES WITH WHITE "SHOULDERS," the area just below the green stem. If it's white, it's tasteless.

SCAN THE SIZE—IT DOES MATTER Very large berries tend to be less sweet. Save the big guys for dishes with sugar (like our Strawberry Sauce, opposite page).

Quick STRAWBERRY-MERINGUE *Mousse*

Purchased meringue cookies add a delicate crunch to this pretty-in-pink mousse.

PREP
15
min

SERVES
4

In large bowl, with mixer at medium-high speed, beat **1 cup heavy or whipping cream** and **2 tablespoons honey** until stiff peaks form. With large rubber spatula, gently fold in **2 cups crushed vanilla or lemon meringue cookies** and **1 pound strawberries,** hulled and sliced.

SKINNY SHORTCAKE *Poppers*

Strawberries are filled with Greek yogurt, then dipped in toasted cake crumbs.

PREP
20
min

SERVES
8

In pie plate, combine **1 slice prepared pound cake,** toasted and finely crumbled, and **3 tablespoons packed light brown sugar.** With small knife, trim stems off **1 pound strawberries;** hollow out centers. Fill with **½ cup plain Greek yogurt.** Dip each strawberry, yogurt end-side down, in crumb mixture to coat.

Strawberry SAUCE

Serve this fruity topping over pound cake, vanilla ice cream—or both!

PREP
15
min

MAKES
2½
cups

In 3-quart saucepan, stir **1 pound strawberries,** hulled and sliced; *½ cup water;* **¼ cup light corn syrup; ¼ cup sugar;** and **pinch salt.** Heat over high heat to boiling, **3 TO 5 MINUTES,** stirring occasionally. Reduce heat to medium-low and simmer **2 MINUTES** or until strawberries are soft. In blender, puree strawberry mixture until smooth. With spatula, push puree through fine-mesh strainer set over medium bowl. Stir in **2 tablespoons fresh lemon juice.** Cool completely.

SUGAR RUSH

TROPICAL
Crisp

Pineapple in the filling and shredded coconut in the topping give this dessert its fabulous tropical taste.

PREP
20
min

SERVES
8

Preheat oven to 350°F. In 2-quart baking dish, toss together **4 cups chopped strawberries, 3 cups chopped pineapple, ½ cup sugar, 3 tablespoons cornstarch,** and **¼ teaspoon salt.** Top with **1 cup granola, 1 cup sweetened shredded coconut,** and **2 tablespoons butter or margarine,** melted; bake **35 MINUTES** or until bubbling.

KITCHEN HACK

Place the butter in a small microwave-safe bowl. Cover with vented plastic wrap and microwave on High 15 to 20 seconds or until melted.

No-Bake PEANUT BUTTER COOKIES

Stash any extra morsels in an airtight
container at room temperature up to 5 days.

PREP
20 *min*

MAKES
24

In medium saucepan, cook **½ cup corn syrup**
with **⅓ cup sugar** over medium heat until
sugar dissolves. Stir in **1 cup peanut butter**
until blended. Remove from heat; stir in **3 cups
whole-grain cereal flakes** until coated. Drop
by rounded tablespoons onto wax paper; cool
completely.

WHITE CHOCOLATE Cheesecake

How to whip up a cheesecake in minutes?
Make it a bar cookie and no-bake easy.

PREP
20 *min*

SERVES
12

Line 8-inch square baking pan with foil. Place
**12 almond thin cookies (such as Jules
Destrooper)** in single layer on bottom. In
large bowl, with mixer at medium speed, beat
1 package (8 ounces) cream cheese, softened,
until fluffy. Beat in **6 ounces white chocolate,**
melted, and **½ cup heavy or whipping cream**
until smooth and stiff. Spread evenly over
almond thins. Refrigerate at least **2 HOURS** or
until set. Drizzle top with **1 ounce semisweet
chocolate,** melted.

White Chocolate Cheesecake

Sneaky Brownies

Sneaky BROWNIES

No one will ever guess there are (gasp!) beets in this dark, dense, and delicious recipe. Look for packages of unseasoned cooked beets in the produce section at the supermarket.

PREP
15
min

MAKES
24

Preheat oven to 350°F. Grease 13- by 9-inch baking pan. In food processor or blender, puree **1 package (8 to 9 ounces) whole, unseasoned, precooked peeled red beets** and **¼ cup vegetable oil** until smooth. Add **2 large eggs** and **1 box (19 to 20 ounces) fudgy brownie mix.** Puree until very smooth. Stir in **1 cup semisweet chocolate chips.** Pour into prepared pan. Bake **25 MINUTES** or until toothpick inserted 2 inches from center comes out almost clean. Cool completely in pan on wire rack.

BLACK-BOTTOM Brownies

Part cheesecake, part brownie, these super-easy squares are definitely worth adding to your cookie repertoire.

PREP
20
min

SERVES
8

Preheat oven to 350°F. Prepare **1 box (18 ounces) brownie mix** as label directs for 9-inch square baking pan. In large bowl with mixer at medium-high speed, beat **1 package (8 ounces) cream cheese,** softened; **1 large egg;** and **½ cup sugar** until smooth. Pour over brownie mixture in pan. Bake **45 MINUTES** or until toothpick inserted 2 inches from center comes out almost clean. Cool completely in pan on wire rack.

KITCHEN HACK

Unwrap the cream cheese, place in microwave-safe bowl, and microwave on High 30 to 45 seconds or just until softened.

Buttery POUND CAKE

Cake flour ensures this cake has an extra-tender crumb.

PREP
20
min

SERVES
12

2 cups cake flour (not self-rising)
1 teaspoon baking powder
½ teaspoon salt
1 cup (2 sticks) butter, softened
1 cup sugar
4 large eggs
1½ teaspoons vanilla extract

1. Preheat oven to 325°F. Grease and flour 9- by 5-inch metal loaf pan.

2. In medium bowl, stir together flour, baking powder, and salt. In large bowl, with mixer at medium speed, beat butter until creamy. Add sugar and beat **5 MINUTES** or until light and creamy, frequently scraping bowl with rubber spatula. Add eggs, 1 at a time, beating well after each addition. Beat in vanilla. Reduce speed to low; beat in flour mixture just until combined.

3. Spoon batter into prepared pan; spread evenly. Bake **1 HOUR**, or until cake pulls away from sides of pan and toothpick inserted in center of cake comes out clean. Cool in pan on wire rack **10 MINUTES**. With small knife, loosen cake from sides of pan; invert onto wire rack; invert again right side up to cool completely.

KITCHEN HACK

To soften the butter, place each wrapped stick between 2 sheets of waxed paper. With a rolling pin, pound sticks several times on each side to partially flatten.

For more tasty cakes, prepare the batter for Buttery Pound Cake, take your pick from these 5-minute flourishes, and bake! All recipes make 12 servings.

PB&J POUND CAKE

Stir **1 cup peanut butter chips** into batter. Spread two-thirds batter in pan, dollop **½ cup raspberry jam** over it, and top with remaining batter. Run butter knife through batter to swirl jam.

TRIPLE-CHOCOLATE POUND CAKE

In small bowl, stir **¼ cup unsweetened cocoa** into **1 tablespoon melted butter or margarine;** beat into batter. Stir in **1½ cups semisweet chocolate chunks.** When cake is cooled, spread **1 cup chopped white chocolate,** melted, on top.

COFFEE–CINNAMON SWIRL POUND CAKE

Tastes even better toasted!

Beat **2 tablespoons instant espresso powder** into batter. In small bowl, mix **¾ cup chopped toasted pecans, ¼ cup packed brown sugar,** and **2 teaspoons ground cinnamon.** Spread half the batter in pan; sprinkle half pecan mixture over it. Repeat.

LEMON–ALMOND CRUNCH POUND CAKE

Stir **1 teaspoon finely grated lemon peel, 1 tablespoon fresh lemon juice,** and **1½ teaspoons ground ginger** into batter; spread batter in pan. Press **½ cup sliced almonds** on top. When cake is cooled, sprinkle with **1 tablespoon confectioners' sugar.**

Pineapple
SHORTCAKES

A tube of refrigerated biscuits means these heavenly shortcakes require minimal prep.

PREP
20
min

SERVES
8

Preheat oven to 350°F. Place **1 tube (16 to 16.3 ounces) refrigerated biscuits** on large cookie sheet. Brush with **1 large egg,** beaten; sprinkle with **2 tablespoons sugar.** Bake **13 TO 15 MINUTES** or until golden. Meanwhile, in 10-inch skillet, cook **4 cups chopped fresh pineapple** and **¼ cup sugar,** stirring often, over medium-high heat **5 MINUTES** or until tender and golden. In large bowl, with mixer at medium-high speed, beat **½ cup heavy or whipping cream** until stiff peaks form. Divide whipped cream and pineapple among split biscuits.

KITCHEN
HACK

Instead of beating heavy cream, sub in 1 cup of thawed frozen whipped topping.

Holiday TRIFLE

This seasonal classic is a great use for leftover eggnog—whether it's fresh, refrigerated, or out of a can.

PREP
20
min

SERVES
8

In large bowl, with mixer at medium-high speed, beat **1½ cups heavy or whipping cream** until stiff peaks form; fold in **⅓ cup eggnog.** Cut **1 frozen pound cake (10 to 11 ounces),** into ½-inch cubes. In 4-quart trifle bowl, layer half of cake; **⅓ cup eggnog; 1 bag (12 ounces) frozen raspberries,** thawed; and half of cream mixture. Repeat layering with remaining cake; **⅓ cup eggnog; 1 bag (12 ounces) frozen raspberries,** thawed; and remaining cream mixture. Top with **½ cup sliced almonds,** toasted.

KITCHEN HACK

There's no need to thaw frozen pound cake to cut into cubes; just use a serrated knife.

Chocolate-Macaroon TART

This three-ingredient masterpiece is no-bake easy.

PREP
20
min

SERVES
12

Spray 11-inch tart pan with removable bottom with nonstick cooking spray. In food processor, with knife blade attached, pulse **1 package (10 ounces) soft coconut macaroon cookies** until fine crumbs form; sprinkle into prepared tart pan. With hand, press onto bottom and sides of pan. In large heatproof bowl, place **1 pound semisweet or bittersweet chocolate,** finely chopped. In 1-quart saucepan, bring **1 cup heavy or whipping cream** to boiling over medium heat, about **5 MINUTES**. Pour hot cream over chocolate and whisk until smooth. Pour chocolate mixture into crust. Refrigerate **6 HOURS** or until set. Top with **raspberries** and **slivered orange peel.**

KITCHEN HACK

If you don't have a tart pan, use a 9-inch pie plate.

CHOCOLATE BY NUMBERS

If you're a chocolate fan, you've probably noticed the number of varieties with the percentage of cacao on the label. The higher the percent of cacao (aka pure cocoa beans), the more intense, complex, and less sweet the chocolate will taste. However, using chocolate with a high percentage of cacao can cause some desserts to curdle or become gritty. So if a recipe calls for dark, semisweet, or bittersweet chocolate, stick with brands that do not exceed 60 percent.

Linzer WAFFLE SUNDAES

Hold the hot fudge! Zap fresh cranberries with brown sugar and cinnamon—and you've got a fabulous dessert topper for waffles (or toasted pound cake).

PREP
10
min

SERVES
4

In 2-quart microwave-safe bowl, combine **2 cups fresh cranberries, 2/3 cup packed brown sugar,** *2 tablespoons water,* and **1/4 teaspoon ground cinnamon.** Cover with vented plastic wrap, and microwave on High **3 MINUTES** or until berries begin to pop. Toast **4 frozen Belgian waffles.** Top warm waffles with **1 pint vanilla ice cream,** then cranberry sauce.

Blackberry ICE CREAM SAUCE

Balsamic vinegar brings out the earthy, wine-like taste of blackberries for a scrumptious dessert sauce.

PREP
5
min

MAKES
2
cups

In medium bowl, stir together **2 tablespoons sugar, 1 tablespoon balsamic vinegar,** and *1 tablespoon water* until sugar dissolves. Stir in **1 pint blackberries.** Serve with **vanilla ice cream.**

NEAPOLITAN ICE CREAM SLIDERS

Start scooping ice cream from the outer edge of the container—that's where it will be the softest. If it's rock-hard, zap it on Medium 10 to 20 seconds, checking every 10 seconds.

Sandwich **4 scoops Neapolitan ice cream** between **8 sugar cookies;** freeze at least **1 HOUR** or until ice cream is firm. Roll in **½ cup chopped pistachios.**

DULCE DE LECHE ICE CREAM SLIDERS

Place **4 scoops dulce de leche ice cream** between **8 sugar cookies;** freeze at least **1 HOUR** or until ice cream is firm. Roll in **½ cup chopped toasted pecans.**

Grab 8 sugar cookies (we like Pepperidge Farm), ice cream, and voila! In just 10 minutes, whip up a batch of fabulous ice cream sliders. All recipes make 4 servings.

S'MORES ICE CREAM SLIDERS

Place **4 scoops chocolate ice cream** and **1 cup mini marshmallows,** toasted, between **8 sugar cookies;** freeze at least **1 HOUR** or until ice cream is firm.

COCONUT-MANGO ICE CREAM SLIDERS

Place **4 scoops mango sorbet** between **8 sugar cookies;** freeze at least **1 HOUR** or until ice cream is firm. Roll in **½ cup toasted sweetened shredded coconut.**

No-Cook
WATERMELON "CAKE"

When it comes to thinking beyond the wedge, this stunner takes the cake. Better yet, it's low-cal too.

PREP
15
min

SERVES
10

Slice 2 short ends off **1 large seedless watermelon** so it sits flat; cut away rind to make cylinder. Transfer to cake stand. Frost "cake" with **2 containers (8 ounces each) frozen whipped topping,** thawed. Top with **strawberries, blueberries, raspberries,** and **fresh mint sprigs.**

KITCHEN HACK

Use a large, sharp knife with a pointed tip to serve the "cake."

Frozen
WATERMELON
COOLERS

Raspberry sorbet and confectioners' sugar make this icy treat thick enough to eat with a spoon.

PREP
20
min

SERVES
4

Spread **4 cups cubed seedless watermelon** in a single layer on small jelly-roll pan; freeze **1 HOUR** or until frozen solid. In large blender, puree watermelon, **5 cups ice cubes, 1 cup raspberry sorbet, 1 cup fresh lime juice,** and **½ cup confectioners' sugar** until thick and smooth (stopping often to tamp down solid ingredients with wooden spoon). Divide among 4 glasses.

Banana
DREAM PIE

Very ripe, brown-speckled bananas are a
must in this recipe (which is equally delicious
prepared in a chocolate cookie crust).

PREP
15
min

SERVES
8

Spread **1 cup dulce de leche** in **1 prepared
graham cracker crust.** Top with **3 large
bananas,** sliced; **¼ teaspoon salt;** and **2 cups
sweetened whipped cream.** Cover pie and
refrigerate, at least **4 HOURS** or until filling is
firm. Sprinkle with **shaved chocolate.**

Nectarine
CUSTARD PIE

Why pick nectarines over peaches for a
speedy pie? Unlike peaches, there's no
need to peel the fruit.

PREP
20
min

SERVES
8

Preheat oven to 425°F. Ease **1 (9-inch)
refrigerated ready-to-use piecrust** into
9-inch pie plate, gently pressing dough against
side of plate; crimp edge. In large bowl, whisk
together **¾ cup buttermilk, ¾ cup sugar,
2 large eggs, ¼ cup all-purpose flour,** and
⅛ teaspoon salt until smooth. Spread **4 cups
chopped nectarines** in crust; add buttermilk
mixture. Bake **40 MINUTES** or just until set.
Cool completely on wire rack.

KITCHEN HACK

If the edge of the crust
becomes too brown before
the filling is set, cover it
loosely with foil during last
15 minutes of baking.

No-Cook
KEY LIME PIE

Lime-loving avocado is the secret to this ultra-luscious filling.

PREP
20
min

SERVES
8

In large bowl, with mixer at medium speed, beat **2 packages (3 ounces each) cream cheese,** softened, and **2 ripe avocados,** pitted and peeled, until smooth. Beat in **1 can (14 ounces) sweetened condensed milk, 1 teaspoon finely grated lime peel,** and **⅔ cup fresh lime juice.** Pour into **1 prepared graham cracker crust.** Cover and freeze at least **2 HOURS** or until filling is firm. Serve with **whipped cream.**

KITCHEN HACK

Take a moment to roll each lime on the countertop. This will burst the segments inside the fruit so you'll get more juice.

226

Easy PLUM TART

Preheat oven to 400°F. Line large cookie sheet with parchment paper. On floured surface, roll **1 (9-inch) refrigerated ready-to-use piecrust** into 12-inch round. Transfer to prepared cookie sheet. Spread **¾ cup canned almond cake and pastry filling** onto crust, leaving 2-inch border. Top filling with **4 to 5 medium plums,** sliced. Fold border of crust over fruit, pleating edges. Bake **30 TO 35 MINUTES** or until crust is golden and filling is bubbling. Cool **15 MINUTES** on cookie sheet, then slide tart onto wire rack to cool completely.

This free-form tart bakes right on a cookie sheet, eliminating the fuss of fitting the crust in a pie plate.

PREP
25
min

SERVES
8 to 10

KITCHEN HACK

Zap the ready-to-use piecrust on Defrost (30% power) 10 to 15 seconds before unfolding and rolling into 12-inch round.

Pomegranate
POACHED PEARS

Firm Bosc pears are perfect for poaching. Their dense flesh retains its shape when cooked, plus their complex spicy flavor holds its own paired with tangy pomegranate juice.

PREP
20
min

SERVES
6

In 4-quart saucepan, combine **4 cups unsweetened pomegranate juice; 6 Bosc pears,** peeled, halved, and cored; **¼ cup sugar;** and **1 cinnamon stick.** Heat just to boiling over medium-high heat, **10 TO 15 MINUTES**. Reduce heat to medium-low and simmer **15 TO 25 MINUTES** or until pears are tender. Cool pears completely in pan on wire rack. Drizzle with poaching liquid and serve with **sour cream** and **fresh mint sprigs.**

KITCHEN
HACK

To test the pears for doneness, insert a toothpick into the thickest part of a pear half; there should be little resistance.

APPLES

If you're a freshman baker and want to make an easy dessert, apples are the teacher's pet.

GO ANTIQUE

Apples that were popular decades or even centuries ago, known as heirloom apples, are widely available at farmers' markets. Now thanks to advances in cold-storage technology, some heirloom varieties are making their way onto supermarket shelves too. Check the produce section for these oldies but goodies that are great for baking.

GRAVENSTEIN This greenish-yellow-skinned apple with light to dark red stripes has a honey sweet-tart flavor with juicy, crisp flesh.

JONATHAN A red-skinned cruncher blushed with yellow to green undertones is popular for lively sweet-sharp taste, crisp bite, and juiciness.

WINESAP A green- to deep-red-hued apple with very firm, super-juicy flesh, and tart-tangy flavor.

PICK OF THE CROP Whatever variety you choose, select apples that are shiny, firm to the touch, have a good aroma, and are free of skin breaks.

Easiest
BAKED APPLES

Using halved apples, versus whole fruit, makes the task of coring and stuffing a no-brainer.

PREP
15
min

SERVES
4

Preheat oven to 350°F. In small bowl, with fingertips, mix **⅓ cup packed brown sugar; ¼ cup old-fashioned oats; 2 tablespoons butter or margarine,** softened and cut up; **2 tablespoons all-purpose flour;** and **¼ teaspoon ground cinnamon** until coarse crumbs form. With melon baller, scoop out centers of **2 Winesap or McIntosh apples,** halved. Place apple halves, cut side up, on cookie sheet. Fill cavities with crumbs. Bake **35 MINUTES** or until apples are tender.

Mom's
APPLE CRISP

Try a mix of tart and sweet baking apples in the filling, like Granny Smith and Golden Delicious.

PREP
25
min

SERVES
8

Preheat oven to 400°F. In greased 13- by 9-inch glass baking dish, toss **3 pounds apples,** peeled and cut into ¾-inch chunks; **¼ cup packed brown sugar; ½ teaspoon apple pie spice;** and **¼ teaspoon salt.** In large bowl, crush **3½ cups cornflakes** with **5 tablespoons butter or margarine**, softened and cut up; **⅓ cup packed brown sugar;** and **½ teaspoon apple pie spice** until blended. Sprinkle over fruit. Bake **30 TO 35 MINUTES** or until golden brown.

KITCHEN HACK

Press each peeled apple through an apple slicer and corer then cut the slices into chunks.

MAPLE *Pudding*

There's no substitute for pure maple syrup in desserts (versus pancake, which is often flavored corn syrup). For even bolder maple flavor, opt for dark, Grade B syrup.

PREP	SERVES
15 *min*	**6**

In medium bowl, whisk together **1 cup milk** and **⅓ cup cornstarch** until smooth. In 3-quart saucepan, heat **1½ cups milk, ¾ cup maple syrup, 1 tablespoon butter or margarine, ½ teaspoon vanilla extract,** and **¼ teaspoon salt** over high heat to boiling, about **5 MINUTES**, stirring occasionally. Reduce heat to simmer. Whisk in cornstarch mixture; cook **2 MINUTES**, whisking constantly. Transfer to 6 parfait glasses; cover and refrigerate at least **4 HOURS** or until cold.

Creamy CHOCOLATE PUDDING

The surprise ingredient in this silky pudding? Avocado!

PREP	SERVES
20 *min*	**6**

In food processor, with knife blade attached, puree **2 ripe avocados,** pitted and peeled; **1 cup sugar; ¾ cup milk; ¾ cup semisweet chocolate chips,** melted; **½ cup unsweetened cocoa; 1 teaspoon vanilla extract;** and **½ teaspoon salt** about **5 MINUTES** or until smooth. Spoon into cups. Cover and refrigerate, about **2 HOURS** or until set.

PHOTO CREDITS

© Antonis Achilleos: 60

© James Baigrie: 37, 177, 215

Corbis: © Atsuko Ikeda/Image Source: 132

© Tara Donne: 111

Getty Images: © Grace Clementine: 210;
© Dorling Kindersley: 67; © Elli Miller: 108

© Hearst: Philip Friedman/Studio D: 7, 90;
Devon Jarvis/Studio D: 43; Lara Robby/Studio D:
144, 186

iStockphoto: 48, 95 middle; © Joe Biafore: 116;
© Creativeye99: 62 (corn), 182; © Tarek El Sombati:
146; © eye-blink: 95 right; © Louis Hiemstra: 232;
© only_fabrizio: 17; © PicturePartners: 154;
© RedHelga: 62 (garlic); © Tatik22: 167;
© YinYang: 104

© Frances Janisch: 158

© Kate Mathis: 19, 22, 28, 34, 44, 53, 80, 83, 87, 88,
92, 94, 96, 118, 121, 127, 129, 135, 136, 156, 165, 172,
175, 180, 185, 198, 206, 221, 227

© Johnny Miller/Edge Reps: 11, 13, 31, 50, 68-69,
70-71, 122, 149, 153, 222, 224

© Con Poulos: 14, 26, 41, 57, 58, 63, 77, 99, 100, 103,
115, 117, 141, 161, 192, 197, 216

© David Prince: 74

© Kate Sears: 21, 47, 55, 73, 79, 130, 213, 219, 231

Shutterstock: 62 (chili), 95 left, 162 both; © Teresa
Azevedo: 62 (cilantro); © Yuliya Rusyayeva: 62 (onion)

StockFood: © Chris Alack: 78; © Crystal Cartier:
234; © Eising Studio - Food Photo & Video: 64;
© Foodografix: 204; © Ulrike Koeb: 181; © Paul
Poplis: 32

© Anna Williams: 25, 30, 107, 112, 142, 171, 187, 188,
195, 203, 209, 228

© James Worrell: 16

INDEX

Note: Page numbers in italics indicate photos of recipes located separately from respective recipes.

INDEX